Collins

You can't re
for A-lev
Literature!

YES

YOU

CAN

and Mark Roberts
shows you how

Contents

Effective revision for English Literature exams

Introduction

It's official: you're an A-level English Literature student. You've done well in your GCSEs and have progressed on to an A-level English course. Congratulations! You clearly have the ability to succeed at this new higher level. It is a step up from GCSE English, but with the right attitude and the right focus there is no reason why you can't do very well in this subject. And a big factor that will dictate whether you excel or struggle is how you approach revision throughout the course.

How would you feel if I told you that, despite your successes at GCSE, the way you revise is probably not as effective as it could be? And that the techniques you're using mean you might struggle to remember the important things you need to know for your exams? You'd be worried, right? And, no doubt, you'd want me to tell you where you were going wrong, as well as pointing out what revision strategies actually work.

Well, you're in luck. In this guide, I'm going to let you in on the secrets of psychology and cognitive science (the study of how humans think and learn). I'm going to show you where most students are going wrong. Then I'm going to introduce you to the study skills that are most likely to help you do brilliantly in your English Literature exams.

Once we've grasped the basics of effective revision, we'll investigate how you can apply these techniques to your English Literature revision.

Along the way, we'll look at each stage of the revision process to ensure you perform really well in this vital subject. I'll show you how I teach my students to master their English revision, as well as giving you examples of what really successful students do to help them towards top grades in A-level English Literature.

Can you really revise for English?

Despite having tasted success at GCSE, my sixth-form students regularly tell me that they find it hard to know how to revise for English. They often find revising for their other A-level subjects much easier. They'll sometimes even say *You can't really revise for English, can you?* This guide will show you why that common belief is wrong. It will show you that all you need is an organised, step-by-step approach to your English revision. So, if you feel like you don't know how to revise, especially for English, you've come to the right place.

Where most students go wrong with revision

How do you begin revising for English? Let me guess. You get out your class notes – from your bulging A4 binder, or annotated-to-within-an-inch-of-its-life poetry anthology – and you re-read them. As well as this, you go back and read handouts and revision guides again. As you read your notes, you highlight the really important information you wrote down in class or the key parts of your handouts and revision guides.

Am I right?

If you do this, you're not alone. But, I'm sorry to say, if you are revising in this way, you might well be limiting your chances of adding facts and ideas to your long-term memory.

Back in 2013, an important piece of research[1] summarised the effectiveness of the most popular revision strategies used by students. The researchers found a big problem with two techniques that students love to use: re-reading and highlighting of notes. These strategies, they found, wasted valuable revision time and didn't really help students remember things in the long run.

So, what's the problem with these two favourite revision methods?

Re-reading your notes doesn't really work

✗ Re-reading your notes doesn't help your understanding of what you read.

✗ Any benefits you get are probably not long-term.

✗ You might remember things soon after re-reading, but you might forget, or not really understand, what you've just read over.

Please let me keep my highlighter!

If your little neon friends make you feel comfortable while reading, then I'm not going to suggest that you stick your highlighters in the bin! But if you're going to use them, make sure you recognise that highlighting can only be the first step of your revision journey. After highlighting, you'll need to move on to techniques that have more benefit.

Does your highlighting look like this?

So what really works when revising?

According to the evidence from cognitive science, the two most effective revision strategies are **retrieval practice** and **spaced practice**.

Retrieval practice involves a test to see what you can remember about a particular subject. Crucially, to do this properly, this test has to be done without notes or other revision materials.

Forcing ourselves us to recall information from memory is a really effective revision technique. When you start doing retrieval activities, though, you might not enjoy them!

To begin with, retrieval practice feels much more challenging than reading over your notes, or highlighting sections of a revision guide. But over time, as you test yourself you'll start to feel more confident.

The first thing you'll notice is that retrieval practice allows you to see the gaps in your knowledge. For example, you might think that you understood a particular poem really well when you covered it in class, but when you quiz yourself without your anthology notes, you discover that you can't remember any quotations.

Secondly, the struggle of remembering information actually strengthens your long-term memory.

Things are far more likely to be remembered if you've had to pluck them from your mind rather than having the answer before your eyes. The effort of putting yourself on the spot really is worth the uncomfortable feeling of not being able to answer questions you thought you could. What's more, researchers have also found that retrieval practice works well in preparing you to remember key information even in really stressful tests.

So, using this technique should help you to recall what you've learnt in the high pressure situation of an exam hall.

Retrieval practice – testing for a better memory

✔ Practice tests can give a big boost to your learning.

✔ All you need is a pen and some flashcards.

✔ It works just as well self-quizzing or paired up with a friend.

✔ You can even create flashcards in class as you take notes.

✔ Feels difficult but helps you prepare for the pressure of an A-level English Literature exam.

What does a good English Literature flashcard look like?

When creating revision flashcards, remember the following tips:

- Include a question on one side and answers or definitions on the other side.
- Double check the answer(s) – you don't want to remember something that's incorrect by mistake.

Take a look at this excellent example:

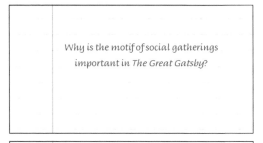

Why is the motif of social gatherings
important in *The Great Gatsby*?

1. Extravagance reveals the obsession with wealth and status
2. Lack of genuine intimacy at these events exposes the shallowness of the American Dream
3. Gatsby's and Tom's parties reinforce differences between old and new money
4. Gatsby's small funeral shows superficial relationship with crowds at earlier parties

How should I use flashcards during retrieval practice?

The most important things to remember when using flashcards are:

- You must include a decent pause before checking the answer. Resist the temptation to flip it over quickly. If you fail to leave a pause while you're thinking, you'll miss out on the long-term memory boost that comes with this technique.
- Pay particular attention to the cards that you struggle with the most. Put these at the back of your pile to ensure that you have another go at recalling the answer. If you still have no idea after two or three attempts, you'll have to go back and check your more detailed class notes, or ask your teacher to go over this with you again.

- Don't forget to go back over the cards you found easy first time. The research suggests that, even with ones you could answer quickly to begin with, there is a clear benefit of testing yourself with them again and again.

Spaced practice is when a student spreads out their revision in shorter sessions over a longer period of time, rather than trying to revise everything in marathon sessions.

For example, you might study a different character from *Hamlet* over a few weeks before your mock exam, rather than trying to study all of the play's major characters the night before.

Students do tend to revise by going over all the information in one long revision session, commonly known as cramming. But the research shows that this is a really bad way to study because the material doesn't move from your working memory to your long-term memory. What's more, cramming is stressful and tends to eat into your precious sleep.

With spaced practice, the opposite occurs: because you are frequently revisiting your learning in small chunks, it is far more likely to stick in the long run and you are far more likely to feel less anxious before an exam.

You'll still need to study the night before an important test, but you won't need to spend hours frantically trying to re-learn something you haven't covered for ages.

Spaced practice versus cramming

An important part of spaced practice is making sure that as well as going back over things that you have studied in the last lesson, you also make sure you revisit things that you covered three days, a week, and a month ago.

Combine this with retrieval practice and you will be using a potent mix of the most effective study techniques.

Start with the older material first. For example, you might have put some flashcards to one side a couple of weeks ago, feeling confident that you had remembered everything on them. Go through them again and see if you can still recall things as fluently as before.

For maximum benefit, revise the material you learn in class throughout the year, not just when you have an assessment on the horizon. Little and often, varying the gaps between when you go back over a topic, is the way to go for the best results.

Spaced practice – gaps between learning to make things stick

✔ Regularly revisiting your learning helps you remember things in the long-term.

✔ Put aside a bit of time for your English revision each day, not just near a test.

✔ Vary the things that you revise and don't forget stuff you haven't done for a while.

✔ Works much better than cramming and is far less stressful!

66 Top 5 to thrive

1. Most students use ineffective revision strategies.

2. Re-reading and highlighting aren't good ways to revise.

3. Retrieval practice feels difficult to begin with but really helps you remember key information.

4. Flashcards are brilliant for revising English, but use them carefully.

5. Space out your revision schedule for maximum impact.

99

Organising your notes and annotations

Students who take notes in class while listening to the teacher typically do better in exams than those who don't. Taking notes gives you a better chance of remembering the content of the lesson. What's more, creating your own notes has a more positive impact on your long-term learning than being given a set of notes by the teacher.

But there's a problem with note-taking.

It seems straightforward but it's actually quite tricky to master.

Listening, picking out the most important information, and writing it down at the same time, can be pretty difficult. And these notes are going to be the basis of your all-important revision schedule.

So it's vital that you learn how to make notes that will be helpful when you come to use them for your revision.

Note-taking in class – common mistakes to avoid

Here are some of the things that can go wrong when you take notes in class:

- Trying to copy down everything on the board.
- Trying to copy down everything the teacher says.
- The teacher talks much quicker than you can write.

When you attempt to copy down all possible information, it stops you listening carefully.

This prevents you getting a good understanding of the main points of the topic. It's easy to see why students fall into these traps: nobody ever shows them how to take notes effectively!

It needn't be like this.

I'm going to introduce you to a note-taking method that will allow you to organise your notes. That will enable you to record the most important ideas and vocabulary. That will give you a better chance of creating notes good enough to use as a basis for your revision. Then, later on in this section, I'm going to show you how a really successful student has taken this note-taking approach to a different level.

Cornell notes – the answer to your note-taking problems

The Cornell notes method was created by Walter Pauk, a professor of education at Cornell University, in the 1940s. Once you get the hang of it, it's easy to use. It may seem simple but it can have a significant impact on the quality of your notes and your overall achievement.

Let's have a look at what you need to do when taking notes.

Firstly, get the right layout on your page:

Step 1: Leave a gap to write the title, topic, date, etc. here.

Step 2: Draw I-shaped lines on your sheet of A4 paper. Use a third of the width for the left column and two-thirds for the right column.

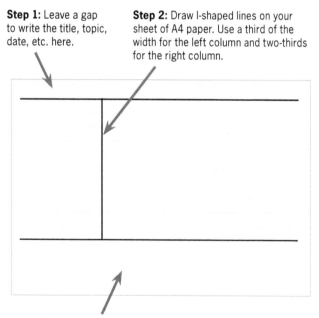

Step 3: Leave a few lines at the bottom for your summary.

Next, follow the method of what to write and where to write it:

Step 4: Write your notes during the lesson.

Step 5: Think of a question that your notes will help you to answer. Use a statement if you can't think of a question.

Step 6: Write a short summary of what you've covered on the page.

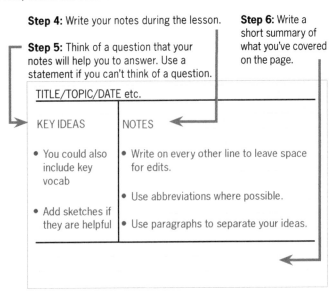

TITLE/TOPIC/DATE etc.	
KEY IDEAS	NOTES
• You could also include key vocab • Add sketches if they are helpful	• Write on every other line to leave space for edits. • Use abbreviations where possible. • Use paragraphs to separate your ideas.

Here's an example of what a page, using the Cornell notes format, might look like:

Beloved by Toni Morrison – settings: 124 Bluestone Rd – 11/2/2021	
What is the significance of 124's location?	No surrounding buildings – conveys geographical and psychological isolation.
Why does Sethe stay in this haunted space?	Being confined in 124 forces Sethe to confront traumatic memories of the past. Offers opportunity to maintain connection and reconcile with Beloved.
Links to popular Southern Gothic tropes?	As a building, 124 reinforces the genre's fixation with history – 124 as microcosm for slavery and the marginalised other.

- Location of 124 mirrors isolation of its inhabitants.
- Confinement paradoxically offers Sethe chance to confront traumatic past.
- The setting meets genre tropes – facing up to the horrors and injustices of the past.

The importance of vocabulary

The central supernatural element of *Beloved*, for example, is the haunting of 124 Bluestone Road ('merely looking in a mirror shattered it'). In traditional Gothic stories, possessed buildings bring fear and suffering. An excellent word for evil spirits that intend to do harm is the adjective 'malevolent'. But by using an innocent murdered baby as the spirit, Morrison flips the obvious haunted house trope on its head. A better way of phrasing this is to use the noun 'subversion'.

Adding these words to your vocabulary list on your Cornell notes sheet should eventually allow you to write sentences like:

> Through her creation of morally complex characters, Morrison subverts Gothic conventions to expose how the society that allowed the enslavement of Sethe forced her into committing an unspeakable act. In reality, the appearance of the malevolent spirit provides Sethe with an opportunity to reconcile with the trauma of taking her child's life.

Continue to apply ambitious vocabulary like this when writing about other texts. Instead of writing 'In Austen's novels women are sometimes able to successfully reject offers of marriage', you can write 'Austen's novels frequently promote a subversion of the trope that persevering men are able to successfully coerce young women into accepting unwelcome offers of marriage'.

How to get the most out of your Cornell notes

I asked my ex-student, Molly Bolding, how she uses Cornell notes. Molly did brilliantly at A-level English Literature and went on to study English at Cambridge University.

Her top tips are:
- Write your ideas out clearly, in full sentences, in the notes section.
- Paragraph properly to separate your ideas out.
- Include plenty of detail – you'll be coming back to this in revision, so the more you write now the more helpful this will be.
- In class, you only need to fill in the notes section. Wait until your revision time to complete the question and summary sections.
- If you can't think of a question, use a short statement – either way, it should prompt you to think of the notes you have written in full.

- Don't include too much information in the question/statement.
- Write your summary section in a different colour. When you're skimming through your book looking for a certain topic, it'll be easier to find the relevant summary.

Using Cornell notes for retrieval practice

Having notes that are clear, concise and organised really helps with retrieval practice. Let's see how the earlier notes page example – focusing on settings in the novel *Beloved* – can be easily turned into a flashcard:

Why is 124 Bluestone Road an important setting in *Beloved*?

- No surrounding buildings – conveys inhabitants' geographical and psychological isolation.

- Staying in haunted building paradoxically comforting as allows Sethe to confront traumatic memories.

- Links to Southern Gothic's historical focus – microcosm for the victimised other in slavery.

But, as Molly points out, if your Cornell notes are really good, you can use them for retrieval practice without always having to turn them into flashcards. Here's how she does it:

Using Cornell notes for quick retrieval practice

✓ Open your book to the relevant page of ideas and read through it.

✓ Cover the notes section with another sheet of paper so that you can only see the questions column.

✓ Practise reading the questions, and either saying or writing out the notes that answer that question.

✓ Don't worry about memorising exactly what you wrote in the notes section, just hold onto the key information or ideas.

✓ Asking yourself what you wrote about pushes your brain to make connections between the key words of the question and those in your notes.

✓ Feels difficult but makes it much easier to recall the information in the future.

Taking your Cornell notes to the next level

Ok, so you've tried out the Cornell notes process. You've now got the hang of organising your notes in this really helpful way. It's also helped with your ongoing revision through retrieval practice.

But Cornell notes aren't just helpful for taking notes while listening to your English teacher in class. Molly also uses them when she is reading other resources – like lesson handouts, revision guides or, most importantly, critical interpretations of literature texts – to organise her notes. She finds these notes just as helpful as the ones she writes in class.

Take a look at an example of how you can use this approach too. Imagine your teacher has given you the following handout to annotate (during a lesson or to read for homework):

Representations of Emilia in *Othello*

Traditionally, directors have depicted Emilia as a plain character, looking old enough to be Desdemona's mother. According to E.A.G. Honigmann, this is a mistake; Emilia should be placed in her mid-twenties and must be attractive enough to lend plausibility to Iago's theory that she has been unfaithful to him with Othello. Either way, it's clear that she is unhappily married. In Cinthio's novella (the original source), Emilia is aware of Iago's plot but is too scared of her husband's wrath to intervene. Shakespeare's Emilia probably keeps quiet about the missing handkerchief for similar reasons. It might also be argued that Emilia is a wife in denial, preferring to avoid being privy to Iago's machinations for fear of what she might discover. As we discover at the play's finale, Emilia has good reason to be wary of her violent, misogynistic husband.

Using Cornell notes to annotate your reading, like Molly, could help you come up with something like this:

Othello – Representations of Emilia – 17/3/2021	
How have critics responded to Emilia?	E.A.G Honigmann: mistake to portray Emilia as old enough to be Desdemona's mother.
Why does this matter?	Adds plausibility to Iago's theory that she was unfaithful with 'The Moor' (I.iii. 369–370).
What's the significance of Emilia's death?	Emilia's death reinforces Kiernan Ryan's comments about violence and misogyny in Venetian society.

- Director's interpretation of Emilia's age is important.
- Younger Emilia makes Iago's belief of infidelity more convincing.
- Her death supports Kiernan Ryan's view on misogyny in Venice.

I prefer to write over the actual handout – how should I annotate?

The key thing to remember, as we saw in the first chapter, is that underlining and highlighting alone is not enough. To end up with decent annotations you can revise from, make sure that you:

- Pick out key bits of information and explain why they're important.
- Summarise and explain ideas and concepts in your own words.
- Write questions and statements, using the underlined/highlighted parts to answer these.
- Write down definitions of key vocabulary, including helpful synonyms.
- Make links to relevant parts of the text.

Here's what this might look like:

How have critics responded to directorial representations of Emilia?

Representations of Emilia in *Othello*

Traditionally, directors have depicted Emilia as a plain character, looking old enough to be Desdemona's mother. According to E.A.G. Honigmann, this is a mistake; Emilia should be placed in her mid-twenties and must be attractive enough to lend plausibility to Iago's theory that she has been unfaithful to him with Othello. Either way, it's clear that she is unhappily married. In Cinthio's novella (the original source), Emilia is aware of Iago's plot but is too scared of her husband's wrath to intervene. Shakespeare's Emilia probably keeps quiet about the missing handkerchief for similar reasons. It might also be argued that Emilia is a wife in denial, preferring to avoid being privy to Iago's machinations for fear of what she might discover. As we discover at the play's finale, Emilia has good reason to be wary of her violent, misogynistic husband.

Why doesn't she take more interest in Iago's plans? (Add this vocab to my flashcards. It means 'being aware of Iago's scheming')

How does Emilia's death reinforce Kiernan Ryan's comments about misogyny in Venice?

IMPORTANT for betrayal essay – Link to 'It is thought abroad that 'twixt my sheets/ He has done my office' (I.iii. 369–370)

Starting your revision of a topic with highly effective notes like these will greatly increase your confidence.

Contrast the notes on page 17 with what you end up with when you just underline while annotating:

Representations of Emilia in *Othello*

Traditionally, directors have depicted Emilia as a plain character, looking old enough to be Desdemona's mother. <u>According to E.A.G. Honigmann,</u> this is a mistake; Emilia should be placed in her mid-twenties and must be attractive enough to lend plausibility to <u>Iago's theory that she has been unfaithful to him with Othello.</u> Either way, it's clear that she is unhappily married. In Cinthio's novella (the original source), Emilia is aware of Iago's plot but is too scared of her husband's wrath to intervene. Shakespeare's Emilia probably keeps quiet about the missing handkerchief for similar reasons. It might also be argued that Emilia is a wife in denial, preferring to avoid being <u>privy to Iago's machinations</u> for fear of what she might discover. As we discover at the play's finale, Emilia has good reason to be wary of her <u>violent, misogynistic</u> husband.

Hopefully, you can see that these lines on the page will be next to useless during revision. You'll have little idea why you highlighted these parts of the text and what you were thinking at the time.

What about annotating poems?

Despite being successful at GCSE, my students often find taking notes on poetry quite tricky. When we first study a poem, they tend to write down everything they learn about it, covering each inch of the page in a rainbow of highlighted colours. Or they write down just a couple of words and end up lacking detail.

For this reason, I think the 'brain dump' approach to poetry note-taking is really important.

Brain dump is a type of retrieval practice where you start with a blank page and simply write down everything you know about the topic you're revising. I find that using this technique with an unannotated poem is a really good way of finding out (a) what you've remembered, and (b) the parts of the poem that you understand the best. An example of brain dump annotation for 'Frost at Midnight' by Samuel Taylor Coleridge might look like this:

My babe so beautiful! it thrills my heart

With tender gladness, thus to look at thee,

And think that thou shalt learn far other lore,

And in far other scenes! For I was reared

In the great city, pent 'mid cloisters dim,

And saw nought lovely but the sky and stars.

But thou, my babe! shalt wander like a breeze

By lakes and sandy shores, beneath the crags

Of ancient mountain, and beneath the clouds,

Which image in their bulk both lakes and shores

And mountain crags: so shalt thou see and hear

The lovely shapes and sounds intelligible

Of that eternal language, which thy God

Utters, who from eternity doth teach

Himself in all, and all things in himself.

The students can now improve and develop these annotations by going back over their original annotations. They can then brain dump again until they narrow down their notes to the key ideas they will need to remember for the exams.

66 Top 5 to thrive

1. Most students find note-taking during lessons a real struggle.

2. Cornell notes help you make excellent notes for retrieval practice.

3. The quality of the notes you take in class will have a big impact on your understanding of topics in revision.

4. You can also improve your annotations while reading handouts and textbooks by using Cornell notes.

5. Just highlighting and underlining is not enough – annotate with summaries, questions and statements.

Building up a bank of 'killer quotes'

Knowing long lists of quotes is great. Being able to remember who said what, what happened when, and which words link to which themes will leave you feeling confident as you enter your English Literature exams.

But while all quotes are important, some are far more important than others. If you select your quotes really carefully, you'll find that you won't necessarily need a massive list of quotes to choose from. If you can identify and understand 'killer quotes' for each text, you'll find that they can cover pretty much everything.

What does 'killer quote' mean?

Killer quotes are memorable, powerful and – most importantly – very versatile. Things that are versatile can be used for many different jobs. Killer quotes are able to cover most key themes. Often, they also help us understand the main characters. Usually, they illustrate important ideas about context as well. In this situation, the word 'killer' isn't anything to do with murder; it is a colloquial term that means 'exceptional', 'amazing' or 'effective'. So, killer quotes are the ones that stand out as the most useful. They're the ones that can help you out with even the trickiest exam questions. Think a Swiss Army knife, but with sophisticated ideas instead of a saw, screwdriver and a tin opener!

Killer quotes – multipurpose quotes for all situations

✓ They're short and easy to remember.

✓ The powerful language allows you to plan impressive analysis.

✓ Structurally significant, they provide lots of links to the rest of the text.

✓ They cover most of the themes so can be used in virtually any exam question.

How can I identify killer quotes?

Here is my five-step guide to identifying quotes that can be used for the majority of exam questions you're likely to encounter:

1.   Re-read the texts and look out for quotes that grab your attention

You may have missed out on particularly significant quotes the first or second time you read the book. Read it again with fresh eyes. There may well be previously overlooked extracts that catch your attention.

2.   Look back through your notes from class

Are there any particular quotes that your English teacher spent ages going over, exploding on the board, linking to different bits of context and other parts of the text? If so, there's a good chance that your teacher thinks that it's worthy of further attention. Discuss this with your friends and your teacher. Are there certain ones that you all end up coming back to?

3.   Scan through your list of quotes for the key themes from each text

Do some of them crop up repeatedly? Might they be used as well as, or instead of, some of your other choices? If they seem to fit most things, they may well be killer quote candidates.

4.   Test out potential killer quotes

Take a quote that you think fits the killer quote category, and tick it off against each theme. Also, consider how it might link to important context. If you've got lots of ticks, you're in business. If not, then it may be a decent quote to use, but it's not killer material!

Check out my example from *Othello*:

Emilia:	
'They are all but stomachs, and we all but food'	
Key theme	**Good example?**
Appearance versus reality	✗
Gender conflict	✓
Racism	✗
Warfare	✗
Betrayal	✓

'They are all but stomachs' is one of my favourite lines from *Othello*. It's such a useful quote for looking at Shakespeare's portrayal of Emilia's world-weary cynicism about the sexual insatiability of men, which contrasts nicely with Desdemona's wide-eyed naivety about how women are viewed by the Venetian state. It uses synecdoche in a fascinating way to illustrate how men like her husband manipulate and consume those they deem inferior. But after I match it against some of the key themes, it gets dropped and discarded, like Desdemona's handkerchief.

Going through your quotes like this is a really useful exercise. Even when you're ruling out possible killer quotes, you're revising your understanding of the quotes and the themes.

5. Check that they match up with other key quotes

One sure sign of a particularly helpful killer quote is that it pairs up nicely with other important quotes from the text. Sometimes, it fits with several quotes on the same focus. When this happens, you can more easily track patterns that are of structural significance in the text. This allows you to write about similarities, contrasts or motifs that run through the text as a whole. By doing this, you'll cover structure as well as language, which is essential in A-level English Literature.

Let's have a look at the following example from *Nineteen Eighty-Four*:

- **'There was truth and there was untruth, and if you clung to the truth even against the whole world, you were not mad'**

This killer quote covers many of the central themes, including psychological manipulation, control of knowledge, power and rebellion, freedom and the dangers of totalitarianism.

Now notice how it links beautifully with:

- *'In the end the Party would announce that two and two made five, and you would have to believe it.'*

And this:

- *'Nothing was your own except the few cubic centimetres inside your skull'*

Then finally:

- *'He had won the victory over himself. He loved Big Brother.'*

Starting with Winston's refusal to submit to the collective acceptance of lies as fact, we can track the motif of individual thought through the three quotes that follow. The first highlights the state's inevitable victory in suppressing dissenting ideas. The second illustrates the increasingly limited space for a person to think freely. The third demonstrates how, through his inculcation by the all-powerful state, Winston finally welcomes his acceptance of untruth and loss of liberty.

Practise doing this with possible killer quotes from the texts that you study. The more links you can make, the more likely they are to be the most useful quotes for your exam.

I still can't find killer quotes. Help!

If you've followed my steps but are still struggling to identify the most helpful quotes, then don't worry. Using some detailed examples from expert English teachers, I'm going to give you a list of very important quotes from the most popular texts that are studied for A-level English Literature. I'm not saying these are the only quotes you need to learn. And I'm not saying you shouldn't build up your own preferred list of quotes. But if you're stuck – or are looking for essential quotes to develop your selection – then this is definitely a good place to start.

Shakespeare

Othello – killer quotes

1. 'Look to her, Moor, if thou hast eyes to see: she has deceived her father and may thee' **(Act 1, Scene 3, lines 288–289)** and 'Look to your wife, observe her well with Cassio' **(Act 3, Scene 3, line 202)**

   - Appearance versus reality is the central theme of the play and these pair of structurally significant imperatives illustrate how both Brabantio and Iago are able to manipulate Othello's perception of himself and the foundations of his relationship with Desdemona.
   - The harmonious rhyme of 'see' and 'thee' almost encourages Othello to scrutinise himself, reinforcing his status as Other.
   - Brabantio sows the seeds of mistrust, while Iago takes advantage of Othello's gullibility and misogyny.

2. 'Reputation, reputation, reputation! Oh, I have lost my reputation! I have lost the immortal part of myself, and what remains is bestial.' **(Act 2, Scene 3, lines 242–244)**
   - The epizeuxis of the first line hammers home the importance of individual status in Venetian society. Without the approval of polite society, Cassio believes his tarnished reputation will live on in infamy long after he has departed.

3. **'What you know, you know' (Act 5, Scene 2, line 316)**
   - Critics have argued fervently about Iago's motivations, yet Iago's refusal to explain his plotting against Othello implies that his victims already possess the knowledge to explain his behaviour.
   - Is Iago hinting that the 'unnatural' pairing of Othello and Desdemona is justification enough for destructive measures?
   - Or is Shakespeare demonstrating that, in life, there are no explanations for malign, vindictively destructive behaviour?

4. **'So will I turn her virtue into pitch / And out of her own goodness make the net / That shall enmesh them all' (Act 2, Scene 2, lines 262–264)**
   - Black and white / dark and light imagery is the play's fundamental motif.
   - Shakespeare's use of 'pitch' implies sheer darkness – as in the idiom 'pitch-black'.
   - Also conveys dirtiness, as 'pitch' is a sticky, tar-like resin traditionally used to coat ships.
   - Iago blackens her righteous name, trapping Othello by recasting her as foul and impure.

5. **'Give me the ocular proof' (Act 3, Scene 3, line 370)**
   - Act 3, Scene 3 is Othello's pivotal scene, where Iago's language of 'pestilence' persuades the 'cuckolded' Moor to take his revenge.
   - Sight is again a key motif – Othello must witness the betrayal for himself, as he clings on to the desperate hope that the allegations of adultery aren't true.

Hamlet – killer quotes

1. **'Who's there?' (Act 1, Scene 1, line 1)**
   - The opening line may seem like a functional interrogative but metaphorically sets the tone for the play's philosophical focus.
   - By conveying uncertainty around Hamlet's identity, we arrive at deeper questions about what makes us human.

2. **'this is the poison of deep grief' (Act 4, Scene 5, line 49)**
   English teacher Patrick Cragg argues that this is the play's best value quote:
   - Hamlet, Ophelia and Laertes are all 'poisoned' by effects of grief.

- Claudius is literally a poisoner, and poisons the ears and minds of the younger generation just as he poisoned old Hamlet.
- Unlike Hamlet, Ophelia is unable to channel her grief into revenge or action; for her, it leads only to madness.
- Claudius recognises how the poison he used on old Hamlet has resulted in Ophelia's madness. But he also sees grief itself as a dangerous and destabilising poison.

3. 'This above all: to thine own self be true' (Act 1, Scene 3, line 78)
   Alice Bloom, English teacher, thinks this is the most important quote:
   - Links to many key themes by raising questions of selfhood versus the state, Hamlet's struggle as an individual and outsider, and metatheatre and performance.
   - That this fatherly advice comes from Polonius is deeply ironic.
   - The duplicitous and pompous Polonius is in reality a cog in the wheel of artifice and corruption that is the Danish Court.

4. 'That one may smile and smile and be a villain' (Act 1, Scene 5, line 108)
   - A timeless aphorism which links beautifully to Hamlet's denunciation of the country under Claudius: 'something is rotten in the state of Denmark'.
   - Hamlet's paranoia and revulsion is illustrated by the diacope of 'smile' and 'smile', exposing the state's sustained façade of corruption and hypocrisy.

5. 'To put an antic disposition on' (Act 1, Scene 5, line 173)
   - Is Hamlet's madness genuine or feigned? In pretending to be mad – performance and metatheatre being, of course, central to the play – does he succeed in driving himself mad?
   - Does the mask of madness poison its wearer, in the same way that Denmark has succumbed to the decay of corruption?
   - Whichever way you look at it, after the pivotal moment where Hamlet adopts the 'antic disposition', his character disintegrates into disturbing neuroticism.

King Lear – killer quotes

1. 'Nothing will come of nothing' (Act 1, Scene 1, line 90)
   - The play's single word motif, 'nothing', seems a simple warning to Cordelia of the consequences of refusing to flatter Lear.
   - Use of epanalepsis indicates a cause and effect structure: shower me with platitudes or lose your inheritance.

- Yet the word echoes throughout the play, reflecting Lear's obsession with loss and absence as he realises the folly of his foolish decision.
- The Fool caustically reminds Lear of his descent into 'nothing[ness]', emphasising how his lack of foresight has left him inferior even to the Fool, who at least possesses self-awareness.

2. **'As flies to wanton boys are we to the gods; They kill us for their sport' (Act 4, Scene 1, lines 37–38)**
   - Conveying the cruelty of his circumstances, and the lack of divine justice, Gloucester's line underlines the constant, seemingly random, suffering that runs throughout the play.
   - By comparing the Pagan gods to malicious schoolboys, Shakespeare offers a bleak and nihilistic take on man's role in the world.

3. **'Into her womb convey sterility! Dry up in her the organs of increase' (Act 1, Scene 4, lines 271–272)**
   - The gods, however, don't have a monopoly on wishing suffering upon the play's characters. In a blistering diatribe, Lear curses Goneril's reproductive organs and wishes barrenness upon her.

4. **'I am a man more sinned against than sinning' (Act 3, Scene 2, lines 59–60)**
   - Later in the play, Lear accepts his 'foolish' behaviour, but still softens it through the alliterative adjective 'fond', which implies his irrationality was driven by an excess of devotion.
   - Yet, throughout the play, a central question for the audience is whether they find it plausible for the eponymous king to perceive himself as mainly a victim.

5. **'See better, Lear' (Act 1, Scene 1, line 161)**
   - In a play about blindness – literal, psychological and moral – Kent's imperative acts as an attempt to reason with his stubborn and myopic master, who cannot perceive the irrationality of his decisions until it is too late.

Twelfth Night – killer quotes

1. **'I was adored once too' (Act 2, Scene 3, line 181)**
2. **'One face, one voice, one habit and two persons' (Act 5, Scene 1, lines 200–201)**
3. **'Love sought is good, but given unsought better' (Act 3, Scene 1, line 156)**

4. 'and thus the whirligig of time brings in his revenges' **(Act 5, Scene 1, line 373)**

5. 'For such as I am, all true lovers are / Unstaid and skittish' **(Act 2, Scene 4, lines 18–19)**

Pre-1900 novel

Dracula – killer quotes

1. 'This was the being I was helping to transfer to London, where, perhaps, for centuries to come he might, amongst its teeming millions, satiate his lust for blood...' **(Chapter 4)**

2. 'the old centuries had, and have, powers of their own which mere 'modernity' cannot kill' **(Chapter 3)**

3. 'When I found that I was a prisoner a sort of wild feeling came over me. I rushed up and down the stairs... I behaved much as a rat does in a trap' **(Chapter 3)**

4. 'At least God's mercy is better than that of these monsters, and the precipice is steep and high' **(Chapter 4)**

5. 'Arthur placed the point over the heart...Then he struck with all his might' **(Chapter 16)**

Wuthering Heights – killer quotes

1. 'My love for Linton is like the foliage in the woods: time will change it...as winter changes the trees. My love for Heathcliff resembles the eternal rocks beneath: a source of little visible delight, but necessary' **(Chapter 9)**

2. 'Let me in—let me in!' **(Chapter 3)**

3. 'Whatever our souls are made of, his and mine are the same' **(Chapter 9)**

4. 'Nelly, I am Heathcliff!' **(Chapter 9)**

5. 'do not leave me in this abyss, where I cannot find you!...I cannot live without my life! I cannot live without my soul!' **(Chapter 16)**

Tess of the d'Urbervilles – killer quotes

1. 'You were more sinned against than sinning, that I admit' **(Chapter 35)**
2. 'Tis because we be on a blighted star, and not a sound one, isn't it, Tess?' **(Chapter 4)**
3. 'it was the touch of the imperfect upon the would-be perfect that gave the sweetness, because it was that which gave the humanity' **(Chapter 24)**
4. 'I was born bad, and I have lived bad, and I shall die bad' **(Chapter 12)**
5. 'though to visit the sins of the fathers upon the children may be a morality good enough for divinities, it is scorned by average human nature; and it therefore does not mend the matter' **(Chapter 11)**

Frankenstein – killer quotes

1. 'Beware; for I am fearless, and therefore powerful' **(Chapter 20)**
2. 'I am thy creature: I ought to be thy Adam, but I am rather the fallen angel' **(Chapter 10)**
3. 'The world was to me a secret which I desired to divine' **(Chapter 2)**
4. 'Of what a strange nature is knowledge' **(Chapter 13)**
5. 'What can stop the determined heart and resolved will of man?' **(Letter 3)**

Pre–1900 drama

The Duchess of Malfi – killer quotes

1. 'We are merely the stars' tennis balls' **(Act 5, Scene 4)**
2. 'Black-birds fatten best in hard weather' **(Act 1, Scene 1)**
3. 'Who am I?…Am not I thy Duchess?…I am Duchess of Malfi still' **(Act 4, Scene 2)**
4. 'if't chance, some curs'd example poison't near the head, death and diseases through the whole land spread.' **(Act 1, Scene 1)**
5. 'The weakest arm is strong enough that strikes with the sword of justice.' **(Act 5, Scene 2)**

Doctor Faustus – killer quotes

1. 'His waxen wings did mount above his reach' **(Chorus 1)**

2. 'Why, this is hell, nor am I out of it' **(Scene 3)**

3. 'A sound magician is a mighty god' **(Scene 1)**

4. 'Cut is the branch that might have grown full straight' **(Chorus)**

5. 'The god thou servest is thine own appetite' **(Scene 5)**

A Doll's House – killer quotes

1. 'You and papa have committed a great sin against me. It is your fault that I have made nothing of my life… I have been your doll-wife, just as at home I was papa's doll-child and here the children have been my dolls.' **(Act 3)**

2. 'The most wonderful thing of all…? [The sound of a door shutting is heard from below.]' **(Act 3)**

3. 'But no man would sacrifice his honour for the one he loves' **(Act 3)**

4. 'I'm no longer prepared to accept what people say and what's written in books. I must think things out for myself, and try to find my own answer.' **(Act 3)**

5. 'To be free, absolutely free. To spend time playing with the children. To have a clean, beautiful house, the way Torvald likes it.' **(Act 1)**

Post–1900 novel

The Great Gatsby – killer quotes

1. 'So we beat on, boats against the current, borne back ceaselessly into the past.' **(Chapter 9)**
   - The beautiful poetry of the ending highlights how humans, in attempting to shape time to achieve their dreams and ambitions, are unable to outmanoeuvre the powerful 'currents' of history.
   - The melancholy tone expresses the inevitability of the enduring spirit of human aspiration ('so we beat on').
   - And yet the alliterative plosives of 'beat…boat…borne…back' – which seem to mimic the sound of the waves slapping us down to our mundane reality – suggests the unfeasibility of achieving our goals.

2. **'I was within and without, simultaneously enchanted and repelled by the inexhaustible variety of life.' (Chapter 2)**
   - Like a moth burned by the bare light bulb, Nick recognises his paradoxical fascination with the vulgar excesses of the decaying American dream.
   - 'Within and without' nods to Nick's liminal state. Constantly present to observe the hedonistic gatherings but considered an outsider by the West Egg aristocracy, Nick offers a perceptive take on the alluring but disturbing indulgences he witnesses.

3. **'They were careless people, Tom and Daisy – they smashed up things and creatures and then retreated back into their money...' (Chapter 9)**
   - In an age of excess and shallow feeling, this quote best summarises how wealth can corrupt individuals to the extent that their default mode becomes moral emptiness.
   - Links to Daisy's 'voice full of money' where Fitzgerald's use of synaesthesia – a key device in the novel – amplifies the couple's privilege and sense of wealth-fuelled entitlement.

4. **'that's the best thing a girl can be in this world, a beautiful little fool' (Chapter 1)**
   - Epitomising Daisy's hyperbolic and knowing shallowness, the superlative 'best' and juxtaposition 'beautiful…fool' sum up Daisy's cynical submission to 1920s feminine norms through the proxy of her daughter.

5. **'"They're a rotten crowd," I shouted across the lawn. "You're worth the whole damn bunch put together."' (Chapter 8)**
   - Having promised to 'reserve all judgements', Carraway is so repulsed by the moral vacuum behind the façade of decency and elegance that he becomes increasingly candid about his feelings for the 'crowd'.
   - Yet, ironically, he is still drawn to Gatsby, a character whose lifestyle is funded by the immorality of bootlegging.

The Handmaid's Tale – killer quotes

1. **'Better never means better for everyone…It always means worse for some' (Chapter 12)**
   - The Commander acknowledges that powerful state regimes inevitably perpetuate inequalities.
   - In an earlier line, Fred Waterford utters the clichéd idiom 'you can't make an omelette without breaking eggs'.

- Through this, Atwood emphasises both his willingness to justify violence as a means to mould Gilead's society, and the lack of originality involved in suppressing female thought and sexuality.

2. 'I used to think of my body as an instrument, of pleasure… Now the flesh arranges itself differently. I'm a cloud, congealed around a central object' **(Chapter 13)**
   - The grotesque stative verb 'congealed' encapsulates Offred's disgust at how her body has been appropriated for the sole purpose of (ironically unlikely) reproduction.
   - Links with her caustic description of handmaids as 'two-legged wombs'.
   - The flesh is personified: such is her dehumanisation and lack of agency that the body feels like a remote 'object' that works independently of her thoughts and neglects her past desires.

3. 'There is more than one kind of freedom, said Aunt Lydia. Freedom to and freedom from. In the days of anarchy, it was freedom to. Now you are being given freedom from.' **(Chapter 5)**
   - Patronisingly dismissive of female independence and intelligence, Aunt Lydia voices Atwood's wonderfully paradoxical 'freedom from'. As a way of describing imprisonment framed as protection, it's a classic example of Orwellian doublethink.

4. 'If it's a story I'm telling, then I have control over the ending. Then there will be an ending, to the story, and real life will come after it.' **(Chapter 7)**
   - As with Winston Smith in *Nineteen Eighty-Four*, Offred's use of the written word has the potential to be a symbolically powerful act of rebellion, a way to emphasise that she, and women like her, cannot be silenced.
   - In narrating her life, she attempts to exert 'control'. Whether her escape to 'real life' is successful is unclear, but we do know for sure that her story does indeed live on.

5. 'A rat in a maze is free to go anywhere, as long as it stays inside the maze' **(Chapter 27)**
   - Reinforcing Aunt Lydia's paradoxical 'freedom from', the zoomorphic comparison with a caged 'rat' highlights the illusion of Offred's liberty, which is in reality controlled by impossibly strict, grossly restricting parameters.

Atonement – killer quotes

1. 'possessed by a desire to have the world just so' **(Part 1, Chapter 1)**

2. 'Something irreducibly human, or male, threatened the order of their household, and Briony knew that unless she helped her sister, they would all suffer' **(Part 1, Chapter 10)**

3. 'imagination itself was a source of secrets' **(Part 1, Chapter 1)**

4. 'This was surely a cynical attempt to win forgiveness for what could never be forgiven' **(Part 1, Chapter 14)**

5. 'a person is, among all else, a material thing, easily torn, not easily mended' **(Part 3, Chapter 4)**

Mrs Dalloway – killer quotes

1. 'Mrs Dalloway said she would buy the flowers herself.' **(Part 1)**

2. 'The death of the soul' **(Part 5)**

3. 'This late age of the world's experience had bred in them all, all men and women, a well of tears.' **(Part 3)**

4. 'priest of science' **(Part 5)**

5. 'I'll give it you!' **(Part 8)**

Nineteen Eighty-Four – killer quotes

1. 'If you want a picture of the future, imagine a boot stamping on a human face – for ever' **(Part 3, Chapter 3)**

2. 'It was a bright cold day in April, and the clocks were striking thirteen' **(Part 1, Chapter 1)**

3. 'We're not dead yet' **(Part 2, Chapter 2)**

4. 'There was truth and there was untruth, and if you clung to the truth even against the whole world, you were not mad' **(Part 2, Chapter 9)**

5. 'Who controls the past controls the future. Who controls the present controls the past.' **(Part 1, Chapter 3 & Part 3, Chapter 2)**

Beloved – killer quotes

1. '124 was spiteful. Full of a baby's venom' **(Chapter 1)**

2. 'those boys came in there and took my milk...Them boys found out I told on em. Schoolteacher made one open up my back, and when it closed it made a tree. It grows there still.' **(Chapter 1)**

3. 'Freeing yourself was one thing; claiming ownership of that freed self was another' **(Chapter 9)**

4. 'For a used-to-be-slave woman to love anything that much was dangerous' **(Chapter 4)**

5. 'It was not a story to pass on' **(Chapter 28)**

Brighton Rock – killer quotes

1. 'It's like those sticks of rock: bite it all the way down, you'll still read Brighton. That's human nature.' **(Part 7)**

2. 'You can't conceive, my child, nor can I or anyone the... appalling...strangeness of the mercy of God.' **(Part 7)**

3. 'He watched her with his soured virginity, as one might watch a draught of medicine offered that one would never, never take' **(Part 3)**

4. 'Hale knew, before he had been in Brighton three hours, that they meant to murder him.' **(Part 1)**

5. 'She walked rapidly in the thin June sunlight towards the worst horror of all.' **(Part 7)**

The Kite Runner – killer quotes

1. 'It may be unfair, but what happens in a few days, sometimes even a single day, can change the course of a whole lifetime' **(Chapter 11)**

2. 'it's wrong what they say about the past... about how you can bury it. Because the past claws its way out.' **(Chapter 1)**

3. 'You've always been a tourist here, you just didn't know it' **(Chapter 19)**

4. 'There is a way to be good again' **(Chapter 1)**

5. 'I became what I am today at the age of twelve, on a frigid overcast day in the winter of 1975.' **(Chapter 1)**

A Streetcar Named Desire – killer quotes

1. 'I have always depended on the kindness of strangers' **(Scene 11)**
   - With bitter irony, Blanche misunderstands the nature of the 'rescue'. Far from assisting out of chivalric politeness, the doctor is the last in a long line of 'strangers' to note Blanche's ever-decreasing grasp of reality.
   - The euphemistic 'strangers' provokes thoughts of the many 'kind' men who have in reality merely shown affection towards Blanche for sex. Her dependence in this regard is tied to her sexual availability.

2. 'I can hardly stand it when he is away for a night…when he's away for a week I nearly go wild!' **(Scene 10)**
   - The intensity of Stella's feelings for Stanley – established in the opening scene's greeting 'Hey there! Stella, Baby!' – are revealed through this passionate, some might say mad, expression of desire.
   - Blinded by a marriage successfully built on sex, Stella cannot accept the reality of her husband's brutalisation of her sister.

3. 'I don't want realism. I want magic!' **(Scene 9)**
   - Driven by a desire for a world of fantasy and artifice, Blanche does all she can to evade the harsh glare of reality.
   - Yet Blanche is unable to shed her actual persona. Given her past 'intimacies with strangers', no amount of mythmaking can persuade the increasingly Stanley-like Mitch to share her delusions.

4. 'Since earliest manhood the centre of his life has been pleasure with women…not with weak indulgence, dependently, but with the power and pride of a richly feathered male bird among hens' **(Scene 1)**
   - Stanley is depicted as a peacock-like creature, ostentatious and bursting with testosterone, keen to consume and dominate the women he meets.
   - The alliterative plosives 'power' and 'pride' form a toxic combination, foreshadowing the consequences of arrogance and excessive lust.

5. 'This game is seven-card stud' (**Scene 11**)
    • The final line is anticlimactic but conveys an ominous mood, which leaves the audience feeling concerned for Stella.
    • The choice of 'stud' symbolises how Stanley's predatorial sexual desire appears undiminished.
    • Masculine dominance, framed through the microcosm of poker, remains resolutely intact. Blanche's yearning for a world of 'magic' has gone, replaced by hard, cold reality.

Death of a Salesman – killer quotes

1. 'You can't eat the orange and throw the peel away – a man is not a piece of fruit' (**Act 2**)
2. 'No man only needs a little salary' (**Requiem**)
3. 'When a deposit bottle is broken you don't get your nickel back' (**Act 1**)
4. 'A small man can be just as exhausted as a great man' (**Act 1**)
5. 'it's a business kid, and everybody's gotta pull his own weight' (**Act 2**)

66 Top 5 to thrive

1. Killer quotes are important because they're the most versatile.
2. Spend time identifying these quotes from your quote lists.
3. Make sure these quotes cover structure as well as language.
4. If you're stuck, use the killer quotes listed above.
5. Link killer quotes to other key quotes on the same theme for maximum effect.

99

Exploding your quotes

You now have a judicious selection of quotes, ready to slay even the most fiendish of exam questions. It's important that you put these on to flashcards, as being able to recall key quotes fluently will mean you don't have to spend ages having to flick through the book in an exam situation, saving you precious time in the process.

Just knowing lots of quotes, however, isn't sufficient. Being able to recall quotes is really important. But knowing quotes is only a stepping stone towards brilliant written analysis. If you're going to fly in your exams, you'll need to have really detailed plans of what you're going to say about the quotes that you've selected and learnt.

What does 'exploding quotes' mean?

An explosion involves an object being blown into smaller pieces. As the object explodes, more and more pieces of it become visible.

So, when English teachers talk about **exploding quotes** they are talking metaphorically. In this case, the phrase is a really helpful way of thinking about key quotes. When you explode quotes, you're thinking about all the important things you can write about. Like an explosion, your annotations will exponentially grow as you focus in on small, but significant, parts of the quote.

Exploding quotes – exploring ideas for deeper analysis

✓ Allows you to plan your analysis ahead of the exam.

✓ Makes sure you don't just know the quote – you know what you're going to write about it.

✓ Helps you work out which quotes you are best at analysing.

✓ Encourages you to fully develop your analysis, helping you get higher marks.

How do I get started?

Grab a pile of flashcards, which you've used to memorise quotes for a particular text. For example, you might pick up a card on the character Ida from the novel *Brighton Rock*:

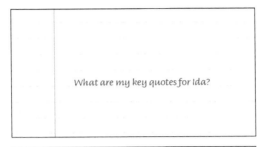

What are my key quotes for Ida?

1. 'She smelt of soap and wine: comfort and peace... a touch of the nursery and the mother'
2. 'It's like those sticks of rock: bite it all the way down, you'll still read Brighton. That's human nature.'
3. 'Fred dropped in indistinguishable grey ash on the pink blossoms...and Ida wept'
4. 'You thought of sucking babies when you looked at her'

Then choose a key quote and start to explode it on a piece of A4 paper, like this:

Powerful and apt analogy – not only does 'rock' imply a hard exterior, it is also a type of sweet that is associated with the innocence of childhood.

Adverbial used to assert that Pinkie's cold-hearted behaviour is not just a surface emotion – like the lettering on rock, evil runs throughout him.

'It's like those sticks of rock: bite it all the way down, you'll still read Brighton. That's human nature.'

Is Greene subtly linking Pinkie's moral decay to the seedy degradation of the setting? Behind the pleasant holiday façade lies a place of deprivation and criminality.

Ida espouses Hobbesian belief that mankind possesses an inherent tendency for pain and destruction.

What kind of things should I pick out?

Just like at GCSE, you need to make sure that you explain the precise impact of evidence from the text. One of the most common errors I see from my A-level students is concentrating too much on context and critical ideas, and forgetting to include close analysis of effect. Therefore, when exploding your quotes, you should aim to make developed notes about the sort of things you'll be expected to write about in your analytical paragraphs.

This might include:

- Language features (hyperbole, euphemism, metonymy, cacophony, antithesis, etc.)
- Key word(s)
- Structural features (foreshadowing, dramatic irony, motifs, exposition, etc.)
- Word class (adjective, modal verb, abstract noun, adverb, etc.)
- Links to theme/context
- Synonyms

Why should I write down synonyms?

A common weakness I see in students' writing is using variations of the same word in their analysis as the key word itself.

This usually looks something like:

> Greene portrays Ida as a wise and nurturing character, who fits our expectations of the maternal archetype. For example, she tries to warn Rose of Pinkie's sadistic and evil nature in the statement 'that's human nature'. The use of the noun phrase 'human nature' demonstrates how Ida believes the evil nature of humanity cannot be altered.

By contrast, a student who reaches for the thesaurus and finds alternative vocabulary for their key words will produce much more impressive analysis:

> Greene portrays Ida as a wise and nurturing character, who fits our expectations of the maternal archetype. For example, she tries to warn Rose of Pinkie's sadistic <u>immorality</u> in the statement 'that's human nature'. The use of the noun phrase 'human nature' demonstrates how Ida believes that <u>mankind's propensity for evil</u> cannot be altered.

Choosing your synonyms carefully

Many words have lots of synonyms, but some of these synonyms are usually far more suitable than others. Synonyms for the word 'touch', for example, include the words 'hold', 'handle' and 'caress'. So if I was intending to use the quote 'She smelt of soap and wine: comfort and peace...a touch of the nursery and the mother' from *Brighton Rock*, I might write down these words as potential synonyms that I could use when analysing the quote.

But beware! Those synonyms relate to the verb 'touch', whereas it is employed in the quote as a noun, meaning a small amount of something. You must be really careful, therefore, to ensure you are using relevant synonyms. A much more appropriate list of synonyms for touch would include: hint, suggestion, scintilla.

If you struggle to think of more ambitious synonyms off the top of your head, you can solve this problem by using a thesaurus. And even if you're someone who has got an excellent vocabulary, your analysis will still benefit from a few juicy synonyms. If you haven't got a copy of a thesaurus at home, you can use an online version. Either way is fine. You do need to be careful, however, if you come across a word you've never heard of. It may be similar to the word you're analysing, but it might not work in the context in which you're using it. If in doubt, make sure you use a dictionary to double check the meaning. In Chapter 7 we'll look at how to use ambitious vocabulary with precision, to make sure your writing is sophisticated but clear and concise.

Compiling a list of effective synonyms

Let's take another look at some of the synonyms I've used in my exploded quote about Ida from *Brighton Rock*:

Powerful and apt analogy – not only does 'rock' imply a hard exterior, it is also a type of sweet that is associated with the innocence of childhood.

Adverbial used to assert that Pinkie's cold-hearted behaviour is not just a surface emotion – like the lettering on rock, evil runs throughout him.

'It's like those sticks of rock: **bite it** all the way down, **you'll still** read Brighton. That's human nature.'

Is Greene subtly linking Pinkie's moral decay to the seedy corruption of the setting? Behind the pleasant holiday façade lies a place of deprivation and criminality.

Ida espouses Hobbesian belief that mankind possesses an inherent tendency for pain and destruction.

Key word/phrase	Synonym(s)
rock	hard exterior
all the way down	runs throughout him
read Brighton	seedy corruption
human nature	inherent

Looking through a thesaurus, I can see that I could have possibly added the following:

Key word/phrase	Synonym(s)
rock	**resilient**, **durable**, brawny, **obdurate** exterior
all the way down	**permeates his being**
read Brighton	**sordid**, **squalid**, low, shameful **degradation**
human nature	**ingrained**, **intrinsic**, basic, innate, **fundamental**

Certain synonyms on my list (highlighted in bold) work really well, so will be added to my exploded quote plan. Hopefully, you can see that dedicating revision time to finding impressive vocabulary will really help improve the analysis.

Synonyms – a vital ingredient for effective analysis

✓ Prepare the words you're going to use in advance.

✓ Reduces the chance of you repeating the key word in your analysis.

✓ Helps you learn and use impressive vocabulary.

✓ Use a thesaurus when you get stuck, or for really ambitious words.

If you prefer, you could make your own exploding quotes sheet to use. Here's an example of what these might look like:

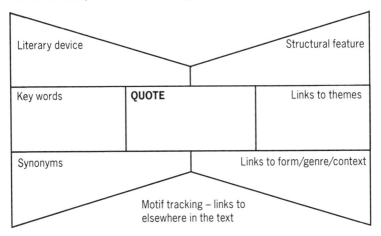

Whether you prefer to use a sheet of A4 to roughly explode your quotes or a template with separate categories is totally up to you. Try both formats and see which best suits your thinking.

Creating exploded quote flashcards

Once you've built up a bank of exploded quotes, you're ready for the next step. You need to ensure that you can remember all the clever things you're going to write about your key quotes. For that, you need to add exploded quotes to your stack of flashcards. Then you can make them part of your daily retrieval practice routine.

Here's an example flashcard, featuring an exploded quote from the play *Doctor Faustus*:

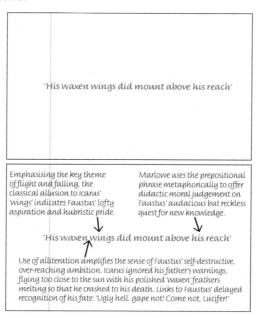

Look closely at the card and you'll see it includes the following:

- Literary device – clear explanation of the precise effect of the allusion 'waxen wings'.
- Key words – detailed focus on 'waxen' and 'wings'.
- Structural features – links to Faustus' later desperate exclamatory statements, building up a pattern of his deluded character.
- Synonyms – above his reach = audacious but reckless; waxen = polished.

It may be improved, however, by including more impressive synonyms, links to theme/context, and analytical and evaluative verbs.

What are analytical verbs?

Analytical verbs are verbs used in your written analysis of texts. These verbs help make it clear what you think a writer is doing and why:

> In 'So We'll Go No More a Roving', Byron employs the phallic imagery of the 'sword' to indicate that in steady relationships sexual desire can dissipate due to overfamiliarity. The 'outwear[ing]' of the sheath implies the speaker has grown tired of a previously harmonious sexual union that now seems dated and incompatible.

Other useful analytical verbs that you could use as part of your planned analysis include:

amplifies	emphasises by adding extra impact
conveys	gets across a message/idea/theory
demonstrates	provides a clear explanation/example
emphasises	draws attention to something
evokes	brings about a strong feeling or idea
foreshadows	hints at subsequent events/themes
highlights	draws clear attention to make it stand out
reiterates	repeats or supports the same point/idea
reveals	makes clear something previously unclear
symbolises	uses something to represent an idea or theme

What are evaluative verbs?

Evaluative verbs are verbs that can take your analysis of texts to the next level. These verbs are really important for A-level students as they show a more sophisticated appreciation of the writer's methods and intention:

> In *Death of a Salesman*, Miller uses the adjective 'exhausted' to examine the notion that material success is attainable for all members of American society, as long as they are willing to strive for betterment. Through his portrayal of the broken dreams of his characters, Miller condemns the harsh aspirational ideologies that have replaced the warmth of meaningful human interaction.

Further vital evaluative verbs include:

criticises	rebukes, admonishes, chastises, lambasts, castigates, demonises, condemns
questions	queries, disputes, casts doubt upon, refutes, interrogates, examines, challenges, exposes
ridicules	mocks, trivialises, satirises, lampoons, derides, parodies, caricatures
celebrates	commemorates, acknowledges, memorialises, lionises, idealises, eulogises, elevates, glorifies, sentimentalises, romanticises
subverts	undermines, overturns, alters, modifies, corrupts
accepts	welcomes, embraces, affirms, reaffirms, internalises, externalises
(technical terms)	hyperbolises, anthropomorphises, zoomorphises

Putting it all together

Having a bank of these exploded quotes makes it much easier when you move on to writing detailed practice paragraphs as part of your revision. Knowing what you're going to write about key quotes will allow you to spend more time in the exam getting your excellent ideas on paper and less time scratching your head thinking about what you're going to focus on and why you picked this quote in the first place.

66 Top 5 to thrive

1. Practise exploding quotes to make sure you can analyse each quote in detail.

2. Make sure you include interesting synonyms for the key words in each quote.

3. Use a thesaurus to help with ambitious words, but double check the meaning.

4. Transfer your exploded quotes to flashcards and make them part of your retrieval practice.

5. Make sure you include developed notes about language, form and structure, and make links to themes and context.

Applying critical viewpoints

One of the challenges of studying A-level English Literature is being able to understand and apply critical interpretations of the texts that you study. Unlike at GCSE English, to do well at A-level not only will you need to use your own ideas when analysing texts, you'll also need to consider the viewpoints of others. To write about texts successfully at A-level, you'll have to write convincingly about the ideas of critics and the theoretical positions that have influenced them.

What is literary criticism?

For as long as humans have performed plays and have produced poetry and stories, others have passed comment on the themes, ideas and effectiveness of their works. Although most literary criticism that you will encounter will have been written since the 20th century, its roots could be said to trace back to Plato and the year 4 BC. These days, most literary criticism is produced by academics working in universities. As part of their role, critics write articles, essays and books about English literature. When done well, they enhance a reader's understanding of a text by introducing new ways of looking at characters, themes and settings, and by offering insights into the relationship between a text and the intentions of its author.

Critical disagreement

Critics often argue about the books that you study. Critic X views the end of King Lear as optimistic, interpreting joy in Lear's belief that Cordelia's spirit will live on in heaven. Meanwhile, Critic Y sees this scene in a totally different way, believing that the end of the play instead conveys Lear's bleak, heartbroken acceptance of his daughter's tragic demise.

As a successful A-level student, you will read and reflect on lots of critical interpretations, thinking about which ones are the most convincing and useful, and making them a key part of some of your essays.

What are critical theories?

While individual critics have their own thoughts about texts, they often write from similar theoretical backgrounds. From the 1930s onwards, big theories about texts became increasingly popular. These theories view works of literature through a particular lens with the aim of illuminating our understanding of people and society in general. Here are some key theories for you to revise:

Critical theory: a very brief overview

Marxist criticism

Karl Marx contended that the purpose of capitalism was to increase profits for the rich through exploitation of working-class members of society. Marxist critics argue that literature should be viewed through the prism of power, work, oppression and money, and should consider whether texts support or challenge existing economic structures.

Psychoanalytic criticism

Making use of some of Sigmund Freud's work on the concept of the self, psychoanalytic criticism applies the central role of unconscious thought to the study of literature and the characters that inhabit texts. Through an exploration of Freud's theories of the Ego and Id, psychoanalytical critics explore the notion of repression, considering a character's unresolved conflicts, hidden desires and responses to traumatic memories.

Feminist criticism

Feminist critics argue that gender is a social construction and that society works to enforce strict expectations about how each gender should behave. Critics from a feminist perspective would highlight examples of female oppression and constriction, using these examples to emphasise the inequality and injustice perpetuated by male-dominated societies.

Post-colonial theory

As a critical approach, post-colonial theory grapples with literature produced in countries that were previously, or still remain, colonies belonging to other countries. It also addresses literature produced by inhabitants of countries that have acted as colonial powers. As such, the theory focuses on key concepts of representations of struggle, racial difference and otherness.

New historicism

Critics writing under the banner of new historicism insist on literary and non-literary texts being afforded the same level of respect. They argue that historical sources, which might traditionally have been seen merely as useful 'background' material, should be seen as important as, and therefore read alongside, classic literature to develop our understanding of both texts.

Writing about critics and theories effectively

As we saw in Chapter 4, when we want to explain the precise effect of a writer's methods we need to carefully choose an appropriate analytical verb. The same is true when writing about a critical interpretation. We need to use a verb that signals the critic's overall point and intention. By selecting the most suitable 'signal' verb or phrase, we can make sure that we write with subtlety and nuance about the exact nature of a critic's point of view. The following is a list of some of the signal verbs that you might use:

argues	puts forward a point of view
asserts	gives a fact or belief with strong confidence
challenges	disputes ideas that have been previously shared
claims	states an opinion that others might consider doubtful
concludes	ends an argument with a particular point
considers	thinks about something carefully or in detail
contends	engages in discussion or debate
depicts	portrays something in a certain way
explains	gives more details to back up a viewpoint
exposes	reveals the true nature of something

insists	makes a point forcefully and repeatedly
introduces	brings in a new idea or concept
maintains	continues to hold the same opinion
notes	draws our attention to something
outlines	explains the main features of an argument or thing
points out	makes an interesting contribution to an argument
questions	queries the validity of a particular belief
reveals	provides knowledge about something unknown or hidden
states	expresses something clearly
summarises	reduces an argument to its main points

Introducing critics into your writing

Using sentence stems can help you to introduce critics effectively in your paragraphs. Here are some that you might find particularly helpful:

* According to [NAME OF CRITIC], ...
* As [NAME OF CRITIC] has pointed out, ...
* [NAME OF CRITIC] famously wrote, ...
* In [NAME OF CRITIC]'s opinion, ...
* [NAME OF CRITIC] has claimed that...
* In the influential book '...', [NAME OF CRITIC] states that...
* [NAME OF CRITIC] challenges the common perception that...

Let's consider what these sentence stems might look like when applied to some popular A-level texts.

Firstly, let's see how this student introduces a critic's idea about the poetry collection *Skirrid Hill* by Owen Sheers, and then uses these ideas to develop their analysis of the text. Notice how, at the end of their analysis, this student skilfully links back to the original critical quote:

> Sarah Crown has noted that, **in *Skirrid Hill*,** 'the ruptured terrain reflects the collection's fractured emotional landscape'. **An example of this phenomenon can be found in 'Winter Swans', where the speaker recalls 'we skirted the lake, silent and apart'. The transitive verb 'skirted' indicates that the pair are literally traversing the edges of the lake. But 'skirted' can also metaphorically imply the avoidance of a painful topic for the 'silent' couple.** As Crown recognises, the 'fracture' **is not just geographical but also psychological.**

Next, here's an example of a student that has taken a general critical interpretation and applied it to a text they are studying, *A Streetcar Named Desire*:

> The novelist and critic David Lodge has written: 'In a novel names are never neutral. They always signify something, even if it is only ordinariness'. I would argue that Stanley's name in *A Streetcar Named Desire* carries great significance. 'Stan' originates from the Old English word for 'stone', which relates to his tough, rugged and uncaring masculinity. Indeed, the etymology of his name might draw comparisons between Stanley and the Stone Age, perhaps giving an indication of his atavistic characterisation. By having Stanley returning home carrying meat, Williams appears to depict him as a primitive hunter gatherer figure.

In this third example, a student has made use of a critical interpretation about *King Lear* and has begun to successfully apply it to a different Shakespeare play, *Twelfth Night*:

> In his influential book *1606: The Year of Lear*, James Shapiro explores Shakespeare's use of single word motifs in the play *King Lear*, arguing that 'each Shakespearean play has its own distinctive music' and the word 'nothing' is 'the motif of Lear's score'. In my opinion, this trope can be applied to *Twelfth Night*, through the example of the frequently occurring word 'mad'...

In this final example of introducing a critical idea, the student effectively fuses a critical quote with the theory that underpins it, applying it to the poem 'Eat Me' by Patience Agbabi:

> Writing from a feminist perspective, Simone De Beauvoir contended that 'One is not born a woman; rather, one becomes a woman'. By this De Beauvoir means that expectations of feminine beauty are dictated by male preferences. The physical form of the female speaker of 'Eat Me' very much fits the category of 'becoming' a woman, as she is literally shaped by the obsessive and abusive fetishes of her male partner. An example of this form of bodily manipulation can be found in...

Evaluating critical ideas

In order to do well at A-level English Literature, you will need to go beyond just incorporating critical ideas into your analysis. Really successful students will introduce the contributions of critics but will then **evaluate** the strength of these critical approaches.

In other words, they will write about which critical arguments they find the most convincing, which parts of a critic's arguments they particularly agree with, and where they feel that other critics have a stronger argument.

By practising playing critics off against each other during revision, you can start to refine your paragraphs so that they will impress any examiner. Here's an example of a student writing about *Hamlet* that shows what this might look like:

> Writing in 1904, A.C. Bradley concludes that Hamlet's treatment of Ophelia is driven by a 'loathing' for his mother's immorality. According to Bradley, 'he can never see Ophelia in the same light again: she is a woman, and his mother is a woman'. Yet feminist critic Linda Wagner has argued that Hamlet's love for Ophelia was never anything deeper than a 'pathetic' Shakespearean plot device. As a character, Wagner insists, Ophelia's presence serves only to 'arouse pity from the audience'. While Bradley might be correct in detecting a sense of misogyny, Wagner offers, in my opinion, a more convincing depiction of Ophelia as shallow love object rather than victim of Hamlet's animosity for Gertrude. For example, in the scene where...

Look carefully at the above example again. You'll notice how the first critic is introduced, then a second critic is used to offer a different viewpoint. Then the student weighs up the opposing viewpoints and makes a decision about which argument they find more compelling. They will, of course, need to support this opinion with evidence, which they will do by analysing relevant quotes from the text.

When you get to the stage of knowing a text inside out and having developed very confident ideas about it, you can start to challenge the viewpoints of established critics. These academics are experts, so you need to be cautious when critiquing their ideas. But if you can question the viewpoints of critics effectively, like in this student's response to *Othello*, the results can be very impressive:

> I am in agreement with feminist critic Jean E. Howard's contention that Othello's disintegration at the hands of Iago 'conforms to derogatory discourse that delineated the Moor as bestial in his lack of reason'. However, I would question Howard's assertion that the process involves a 'gradual transformation'. Most of the eponymous general's fragmentation is far from 'gradual', occurring within a few hundred lines of Act 3, Scene 3: the fulcrum point of the play, where Othello's seemingly strong faith in Desdemona is corrupted.

Memorising critical quotes

A-level exams are usually open book. So while memorising quotes from the texts is still a very good time-saving idea, unlike at GCSE it isn't absolutely essential. But memorising critical quotes is something that you will have to do. Here is the best way to memorise critical quotes:

STEP 1: Create a bank of flashcards

Over time, you'll need to create a set of flashcards for key critics of each text that is assessed on critical interpretations. As you do this, transfer your list of quotes on to flashcards like this:

What are my key critical quotes
for *King Lear* as tragedy?

---

1. The ending 'does not seem at all inevitable. It is not even satisfactorily motived' A.C. Bradley
2. 'the tragic element has been superseded by the grotesque. The grotesque is more cruel than tragedy' Jan Kott
3. 'Like Lear, Gloucester has to undergo intense suffering before he can identify with the deprived' Jonathan Dollimore
4. Lear's 'unique distinction among tragic heroes is that he dies pointing away from himself' Ewan Fernie

STEP 2: Narrow down to shorter quotes

Sometimes, when we're trying to learn critical quotes, we fall into the trap of trying to memorise really long chunks of text. In some cases, short phrases can do a really powerful job, as well as being easier to memorise.

For example, these short critical quotes are really useful for *Othello*:

- Othello tries to 'Europeanise himself' – Andrew Hadfield
- Othello goes from 'honorary white' to 'total outsider' – Ania Loomba
- Iago's 'motiveless malignity' – Samuel Taylor Coleridge
- Iago is 'pathologically normal' – Kiernan Ryan
- Desdemona is 'helplessly passive' – A.C. Bradley

Using shorter quotes will ensure that memorising critical quotes shouldn't be too difficult or too stressful. Make sure you use these flashcards frequently, mixing up the texts you study, and coming back to them at regular intervals.

With frequent practice, writing about critics needn't be too daunting. Using, applying and challenging the ideas of others will, over time, become something that feels like second nature. Keep adding layers of sophistication and, who knows, one day you might become a quoted critic yourself!

66 Top 5 to thrive

1. Make sure you have an understanding of the key ideas of different critical theories.

2. Use appropriate signal verbs and helpful sentence stems to introduce critical ideas.

3. As well as applying critical ideas, evaluate how convincing they are.

4. Use flashcards and retrieval practice to memorise your critical quotes.

5. Shorter quotes are really helpful – use them as a way of memorising lots of relevant quotes.

Using context successfully

At various points in the literature exams, you will be expected to write about context. Different exam boards have different ways of focusing on context in the mark scheme. But one thing's for sure: it's hard to write a decent response about a book or poem that you've studied without having a solid understanding about who wrote it, when they wrote it, and why they wrote it.

So, context matters.

And for that reason, you'll hear your English teacher talk about it lots. But, when they're using this vague term, what do they actually mean?

What exactly is 'context'?

In simple terms, context is the background to the text that you're studying. Typically, when we talk about the context of a novel, play or poem, we often focus on things like:

- When the text was written.
- The importance of the setting.
- What society was like at that time (historical events, attitudes to religion and science, political movements, gender relations, etc.).
- How interpretations of the text have changed over time.
- The writer's background and influences.
- How other writers from the genre may have affected the writing of the text.
- The significance of the writer's other works.
- For plays, how different versions have been performed.

Coping with context

Reading that list, you're probably thinking that's a lot of background information! If so, you're not alone.

My students often struggle with applying context. Particularly when it comes to older texts, like Shakespeare. Written over 400 years ago, there are so many different interpretations about what was going on at the time, and what Shakespeare was trying to say. No wonder my students aren't always sure what to include, and how to include it.

But don't worry. After I've shown them how to use context, they soon get better at applying it to their answers.

And, in this chapter, I'm going to show you how to make sure you use context appropriately and effectively, as part of your revision schedule. I'll explain how being selective in the context that you use will help you to write about it in a way that is clear, thoughtful and, crucially, relevant to the question.

Where most students go wrong with context

When it comes to context, there's a fine line between too little and too much. If you don't understand important background information, you won't really understand the text.

But if you write too much about background, you can drift away from the text itself, and fail to answer the question properly. Based on my experience, and exam board feedback, here's what can go wrong when it comes to context:

Writing about context: 8 common mistakes to avoid

✗ Not including any context.

✗ Too much context.

✗ Mixing up historical events or periods.

✗ Vague references to the past.

✗ Missing opportunities to write about genre or themes.

✗ Generalisations and simplifications.

✗ 'Bolt-on' context that isn't linked to themes, language or the question.

✗ Focusing mainly on writers' biographical details.

For each of these common context mistakes, I'll give you an example of what this might look like. Then I'll show you how you can work to overcome these problems during revision.

1. Not including any context

Imagine you get the following exam question: Explore how Chaucer uses comedy to make serious points about relationships in *The Wife of Bath's Tale*.

This question offers plenty of opportunities to write about the portrayal of marriage, as well as other relationships such as masters and servants. But it would be really difficult to answer this question successfully without making reference to the role of oral tradition as a medieval form of entertainment, along with an appreciation of the significance of court life. In addition, it would be helpful to consider whether medieval moral values are still relevant to a contemporary audience.

Solution: If you find yourself with big context gaps in your essays, go back to your exploded quotes and add relevant context on your flashcards. Use your class notes if necessary.

For example, The Wife of Bath's dialogue 'For sothe I wol nat kepe me chaast in al' rejects traditional notions of courtly love and subversively celebrates the sexual opportunities offered by further marriage.

2. Too much context

But you also need to remember that you are studying for a literature exam, not a history exam. For that reason, context needs to be selective. On that type of question, contextual details might only make up 20% of the marks. So, an answer that spends all its time focusing on the conventions of chivalric romance isn't going to do well.

Solution: Look carefully at the balance of the paragraphs you write as part of your revision. You'll still need to spend most of your time looking at the presentation of key characters, settings and themes, as well as analysing structure and language, such as the adjective 'chaast' from the quote above.

3. Mixing up historical events or periods

I've lost count of the number of times I've seen Dorian Gray and Mr Gradgrind described as characters from the Elizabethan era. Or have read about a Victorian audience's response to Prospero or Petruchio.

Mistakes can happen in exams, but I often get the sense that this is a revision issue. Students get mixed up because they struggle to understand the difference between historical periods, seeing literary texts as all coming from the distant past.

Solution: If you struggle with remembering key periods, make yourself a timeline, which can be added to your retrieval practice. In this example, a student who is studying *Othello*, John Keats, *Dracula*, *A Streetcar Named Desire*, Edexcel's *Poems of the Decade* poetry anthology and *The Little Stranger* has started mapping out key dates and periods:

1603–1604
(Jacobean period)
Othello

1816–1821
(Romanticism)
John Keats

1897
(late Victorian Gothic)
Dracula

1947
(post-WW2 new America)
A Streetcar Named Desire

2001–2010
(modern poetry)
Poems of the Decade

2009
(modern Gothic)
The Little Stranger

4. Vague references to the past

In exams, students often write things like 'in those days' or 'at that time'. Statements like this sound vague and unconfident about dates and historical periods. With some texts, however, the background context is too complex to just link to a certain publication date. Take the novel *Atonement* for example. Published in 2001, it is set in three different time periods: the summer of 1935, during the Second World War (1940), and the 'present day' of 1999.

Some poems about World War 1, such as Wilfred Owen's 'The Sentry', were written during the war based on the poet's experience. Others, like Ted Hughes' 'Six Young Men' (1956) – which uses a persona to imagine what trench warfare must have been like – were published many years later.

Solution: Practise writing sentences that make it clear which period you're referring to. Ensure your timeline reflects the more complicated historical context of some texts.

5. Missing opportunities to write about genre or recurring themes

Students often believe that context is just about what was going on when the book was written, or is set. But, as the list at the start of this chapter shows, there's far more to it than that. Done well, writing about genre or recurring themes is a really good way to place the text you're studying into a wider context.

Solution: Dedicate part of your revision schedule to learning about genre, then practise applying these ideas to your analysis of exploded quotes.

For example, if you're studying a dystopian text, like *Nineteen Eighty-Four*, *The Handmaid's Tale* or *Fahrenheit 451*, you should spend some of your revision time looking at how your text uses dystopian tropes. A trope is a common idea or motif that crops up repeatedly in a particular genre.

This student's example is from *Nineteen Eighty-Four*:

Dystopian trope	Example from text
Use of Everyman archetype	'In the face of pain there are no heroes, no heroes, he thought over and over'
Urban decay	'at present the electric current was cut off during daylight hours'
Oppressive, dehumanising government	'Nothing was your own except the few cubic centimetres inside your skull'
Constant surveillance	'It was one of those pictures which are so contrived that the eyes follow you about when you move'
Threat of violence	'If you want a vision of the future, imagine a boot stamping on a human face — forever'

But what might this look like as a practice paragraph?

> Through his portrayal of Winston as a weak and despondent character, Orwell encourages the reader to identify with him as an archetypal Everyman figure. Indeed, as this dystopian genre trope dictates, Winston's grim ordinariness paradoxically adds to his appeal as a character. Orwell highlights his protagonist's inability to withstand torture through the repetition 'In the face of pain there are no heroes, no heroes, he thought over and over'. The epizeuxis of 'no heroes, no heroes' hammers home the point to readers that, if faced with the full extent of totalitarian power, they too would in all likelihood be continually crushed and left unheroically cowed.

The impressive thing about the practice paragraph above is that it goes beyond just identifying the dystopian trope used by Orwell. It makes sure that it links the trope to Orwell's language and the specific themes of the novel.

6. Generalisations and simplifications

Students often take a general idea about the past and end up making sweeping comments about everyone from that era. They overgeneralise by doing things like making blanket statements about the nature of patriarchal power in a particular period, suggesting that the experiences of all women were identical at that time. Or they fail to take into account differences between Protestant and Catholic faith when writing about religious life in Elizabethan England. Or they make naïve assumptions about the 'freedom' experienced by ex-slaves at the end of the American Civil War.

A classic example I see when reading essays about Shakespeare plays is the straightforward application of Aristotelian (ancient Greek) tragic conventions to his dramas. This leads students to write things like:

> Othello's hamartia is his susceptibility to jealousy, a moral weakness that leads him to kill his beloved because he is primed to accept Iago's lies. This fatal flaw proves his undoing in the end.

There are a couple of things about this reading that are simplistic:

- Ancient Greek drama was far more interested in plot than character. The idea of hamartia or the 'fatal flaw' was seen as an error of judgement that drove the plot, rather than a moral failing causing the hero's downfall.
- In trying to find one flaw that explains the hero's tragic decline, students usually end up simplifying the nature of Shakespeare's characters. This is a mistake; in reality, his characters are defined by their moral complexity.

Solution: Make sure you have a solid understanding of historical facts about setting and genre and that your statements are carefully phrased. Don't assume that people from a particular time all acted and thought alike!

Also, remember that characters are fictional and are often extreme examples, created for the purpose of narrative conflict. Practise writing paragraphs that take these ideas into account:

> Shakespeare uses synecdoche to convey the crudeness of Roderigo's racially stereotypical description of Othello as 'the thick lips'. In reducing Othello to being defined by his appearance, Shakespeare appears to pander to anti-black Elizabethan attitudes. In 1601, for example, Elizabeth decreed that there were 'too manie...blackmoores' and that these 'kinde or people' should be expelled from England. Using this historical fact as an indication of widespread antipathy to those deemed 'other', however, would be a simplistic error. Honigmann has noted, for example, the respectful reaction, in 1600, to the Moorish ambassador, who perhaps provided Shakespeare with 'a model of an aristocratic Barbarian'. With this in mind, we might be tempted to see the 'lips' barb more as articulation of Roderigo's racist resentment against Othello rather than generalising about endemic bigotry in the Elizabethan Court.

7. 'Bolt-on' context that isn't linked to themes, language or the question

As far as examiners are concerned, this is the most common context mistake of all. But what do we mean by 'bolt-on'? When we make a machine, we screw on different parts, bolting separate bits on as we go. When students use 'bolt-on' context, it means that they are adding it on at the end, without carefully linking it to themes, language or the question. Paragraphs in English aren't machines! They need all the elements to be woven together like a wooden basket, rather than sticking in separate sections that don't fit.

Here's an example paragraph of bolt-on context, with an explanation of what's gone wrong:

This part of the paragraph is taking shape: it has started to look at the writer's methods and has successfully introduced the poem's key idea. ✓	In 'The Tyger', the speaker's rhetorical question 'What immortal hand or eye/Could frame thy fearful symmetry?' celebrates the sublime power of the beast, yet questions how a benevolent creator could allow evil to exist in the world.
This part is bolt-on context. The biographical information is correct. But the ideas don't match with the ideas and language in the opening part. ✗	Blake expressed a marked antipathy towards organised religion. For Blake, the one true God was the power of the human imagination.

As part of your revision, you need to work on making sure your context fits with the other parts of your analysis. If in doubt, ask your teacher.

So what might a good example of this look like? Here the student has decided to apply this context to a different poem by William Blake:

The content is directly relevant to the original point and the analysis of language. ✓	In 'Holy Thursday (Songs of Innocence)', Blake's phrase 'their innocent faces clean' uses the imagery of 'faces clean' to illustrate the speaker's disdain for the religious establishment's annual gesture of charity repackaged as propagandising theatre. Through the metaphorical adjective 'clean', Blake suggests that,
The student develops the context, then links back to the quote. This makes sure the information about Blake's beliefs is fully integrated. ✓	in scrubbing up the destitute children for one day, the Church and charitable institutions are complicit in offering a misleading, sanitised vision of the poverty of the abandoned youths. Despite his strong belief in the Bible, Blake expressed a marked antipathy towards organised religion. For Blake, the Church of England was a hypocritical institution. It possessed prodigious wealth but, beyond showcase occasions, did little to improve the lives of the 'innocent' children. By satirising the disingenuous presentation of the temporarily 'clean' children, Blake lifts the veil on the clergy's staged and hypocritical approach to child poverty.

8. Focusing mainly on writers' biographical details

In the William Blake example above, the student uses one of the poet's personal beliefs as a way of illuminating their analysis of a text. When done like this, it can work really well.

But, as examiners are quick to complain, biographical details are often used badly. In essays, students frequently include interesting but irrelevant facts about writers' private lives, which tend to be dropped in without being linked to the question. Juicy gossip about Philip Larkin's affairs with women, or Tennessee Williams' sexuality, might be entertaining but unless tied to the specifics of the question they add little to our appreciation of the writer's methods and intentions.

Often, a focus on how literary or social influence have shaped writers is far more profitable, as can be seen from the example below:

This example starts with relevant context, rather than bolting it on at the end. ✓	In February 1815, Mary Shelley was left distraught after the death of her unnamed 12-day-old baby. Through her portrayal of early childhood, Shelley raises complex questions about the role of fate and agency in human creation. On a surface level, the line 'their child, the innocent and helpless monster bestowed on them by Heaven' illustrates Victor's good fortune in being gifted by a benign creator to a stable and loving family. Yet, on a deeper level, the oxymoronic and dysphemistic 'helpless monster' foreshadows Victor's later hubris in bypassing divine intervention to bring life to his own creature.
The student develops the context and again specifically links it back to the close analysis of language. ✓	Given that Shelley herself had suffered the misfortune of seeing her own 'innocent and helpless' child die shortly before writing the first edition, we might consider how this traumatic incident might have influenced her characterisation of Victor. In creating a character capable of 'bestow[ing]' life without the maternal birth process, then by having Victor reject the 'helpless monster' Shelley could well have distilled her own grief into the creature's feelings of abandonment.

66 Top 5 to thrive

1. As part of your revision, consider the different types of context you can use.

2. Think about what context will be relevant to which questions.

3. Make sure you have the right balance: avoid including too much or too little context.

4. Improve your knowledge of the time periods, and genre tropes, to avoid incorrect or vague statements.

5. Practise writing paragraphs – using my examples as a model – to ensure your context is always relevant and blends in smoothly with your analysis.

99

Developing your academic writing

7

If you're going to be successful at A-level English Literature, a key area to work on during revision is your writing style. Compared to GCSE, examiners at A-level will be less forgiving of clumsy phrasing and sloppy mistakes. You'll be expected to write in a more sophisticated academic manner but, crucially, your writing will need to be fluent and easy to understand. Based on feedback from examiners, and my own experience of teaching students to write much more effectively, here are my top ten strategies for confident, clear and coherent academic writing.

Ten top techniques to improve your academic writing

✓ Signal that you are answering the question

✓ Write about characters as constructs

✓ Don't narrate – analyse

✓ Use cautious language

✓ Avoid phrasal verbs

✓ Cut out wasteful words

✓ Be clear and concise

✓ Make use of nominalisation

✓ Include appositives

✓ Vary sentences with participle phrases

For each of these important techniques, I'll show you an example of where students frequently go wrong when writing English essays. Then I'll show you what you can do to make sure you banish your writing demons during revision!

1. Signal that you are answering the question

Having marked a lot of A-level essays, and having read countless examiner reports, I can reveal to you the biggest flaw in students' academic writing: not answering the question properly.

The reasons why students fail to answer questions effectively are numerous. It can be down to poor planning, dodgy question choice or a lack of knowledge about the text. But many of the problems with responding to a question unsuccessfully are caused by poor writing techniques. Let's take a look at the example below, written in response to the question 'Explore the importance of the relationship between Stella and Stanley in *A Streetcar Named Desire*'. Here are some of the phrases a student has used to try to answer the question:

- From the outset, Stella and Stanley's **relationship is presented as being based on sensuality and sexual attraction**...
- Stella is depicted as a character who finds Stanley's atavistic behaviour, such as hurling raw meat at her, as **an unappealing aspect of their relationship** and yet she cannot help but feel amused by, and attracted to, his primitive behaviours...
- Despite Stanley being the perpetrator of disturbing domestic violence ('the sound of a blow. Stella cries out'), **the marriage is paradoxically portrayed as successful**...
- The arrival of Blanche acts as the play's inciting incident; **from this scene onwards the relationship between Stella and Stanley is under serious threat**...
- Stella's pregnancy makes it clear that **the couple enjoy continuous sexual activity**, despite the presence of Blanche and despite Stanley's acts of violence...
- At the end of the play, **Stella prioritises the marriage over the welfare of her own flesh and blood**, arguing that she 'couldn't believe' Blanche's 'story'. The audience are left understandably concerned for Stella, who appears so besotted by Stanley that she might be so deluded about his behaviour that she is putting herself in further danger...

The student has structured their essay to make it clear they are focusing on the theme of relationships. They use synonyms, such as 'marriage' and 'the couple', to remind the examiner they are sticking to the question.

Nonetheless, there is a problem with this essay: they haven't focused on another key word in the question: 'importance'. For that reason, while the essay analyses some aspects of the marriage, it fails to properly evaluate the *significance* of this relationship in the play as a whole. Let's take a look at how this could be re-written to signpost to an examiner that the student is carefully addressing both key words in this question:

- Despite Stanley being the perpetrator of disturbing domestic violence ('the sound of a blow. Stella cries out'), **Williams portrays the marriage as paradoxically successful. Indeed, in depicting a relationship that isn't even ended by physical assault, Williams foreshadows the tragic ending for Blanche, by revealing the extent to which Stella is unwilling to do anything that risks losing Stanley**...

2. Write about characters as constructs

Another major flaw that crops up in some students' work is writing about characters as if they are real people, like in this example about *Dracula*:

> During his captivity, Jonathan Harker becomes increasingly effeminate. Followed, imprisoned and assaulted, Jonathan sits down and cries 'tears of bitter disappointment'. Powerless before the supernatural force of his captors, his behaviour seems increasingly effeminate with each moment he spends trapped in the castle.

Instead, successful academic writing will recognise that characters are *constructs*. By this we mean that they are fictional entities *created* by an author to help reveal some deeper point about what it means to be human. For this reason, you need to practise writing in a way that recognises this. As you can see from the amended version of the student's work below, as well as sounding more sophisticated, it makes the writing much more focused on the writer's intentions, and on what a character represents rather than does:

> Through his presentation of his protagonist's **captivity**, Stoker subverts Gothic tropes by portraying **Jonathan Harker as increasingly effeminate**. Traditionally, it is a vulnerable Gothic heroine who is **followed, imprisoned and assaulted**. However, in *Dracula*, Stoker characterises **Jonathan as a broken man who sits down and cries 'tears of bitter disappointment'**. By presenting Harker as **powerless before the supernatural force of his captors**, Stoker taps into fin de siècle concerns about the weakening of masculine identity.

3. Don't narrate – analyse

A further issue with the first *Dracula* example above is that, as well as writing about Jonathan Harker as if he's a real person, it also spends too much of the time narrating what happens, as opposed to analysing Bram Stoker's methods.

A-level examiners frequently note that too many essays become very narrative in nature. Like the following example, it means that chunks of their responses focus on re-telling the plot at length instead of picking apart the writer's craft:

> Mephastophilis informs Faustus that hell is a terrible place but, nonetheless, Faustus is willing to sacrifice his soul to Lucifer to gain twenty-four years of service from Mephastophilis. This audacious offer is accepted. While Faustus spends some time reflecting on the life-changing decision to meddle with the forces of evil, he reaches a decision. Ominously, the deal is signed with his blood. For Faustus there is no turning back.

The worst thing about writing in this descriptive manner is that it's a total waste of time. Examiners know the plot inside out, so re-capping in this way is unnecessary and gains very few marks. A far more productive piece of analysis would look like this:

> Marlowe depicts Faustus as a character who is willing to exchange his soul for a corrupt form of power and knowledge. The disturbing dialogue 'with my proper blood/Assure my soul to be great Lucifer's' confirms Faustus's acceptance of the deal. Specifically, 'blood' symbolises the very essence of his being, as well as foreshadowing the inevitable pain of his downfall. Marlowe uses the grotesque imagery of the congealed 'blood' to signal to the audience that Faustus's own body is attempting to reject this terrible pact. Yet, in portraying Faustus as a character who refuses to heed the warnings of his conscience, Marlowe poses complex questions about the role of free will in human thought.

4. Use cautious language

One of the paradoxes of successful academic writing is that the most confident students know when to let examiners know when they're not 100% sure about what they're writing. It may seem odd but being too confident about your ideas and opinions can make your writing less impressive. Conversely, writing in a way that is cautious and expresses doubt – known as hedging language – is much more appealing and convincing to a marker. We'll consider this in more detail when we look at unseen texts in Chapter 9. But here's one example of an overconfident student who ends up making careless comments on a text:

> In 'White Writing' by Carol Ann Duffy, the speaker demonstrates that despite not being legally recognised love can be just as powerful and passionate. The anaphoric reference 'I write them white' evokes a sense of innocence and purity. For this reason, it is clearly an allusion to the expectation that brides will remain virgins until they are married. Therefore, the speakers will definitely not share sexual intimacies until their love can be accepted by the laws of the land.

The language of this response ('is clearly' and 'definitely') places a great deal of certainty on an interpretation that is not supported by the context of the text and is therefore highly dubious. If you're aiming for more original interpretations of a text – and if in doubt it's always best to check with your teacher – it is far better to be cautious in your language:

> In 'White Writing' by Carol Ann Duffy, the speaker demonstrates that despite not being legally recognised love can be just as powerful and passionate. The diacopic repetition 'palm against palm' evokes a sense of unity and lasting devotion. Perhaps here, we can detect a Shakespearean allusion to the first meeting between Romeo and Juliet, who place their 'palms' together as a kissing substitute, a way of sharing a hidden intimacy. It could be argued that, like the famous young lovers, the speaker's love is also forbidden. Yet, in resting 'palm against palm' the couple in 'White Writing' appear to share a similar tenderness and rebelliousness as Romeo and Juliet.

5. Avoid phrasal verbs

Phrasal verbs are phrases that are commonly used in spoken language. But because these phrases are colloquial, we need to get rid of them when writing academically. Take a look back at my use of 'get rid of' in the last sentence, for example. As this book isn't an academic essay, it is fine for me to use informal, chatty phrases like that. But when I'm writing academically, I'd avoid using phrasal verbs like 'get rid of' (or 'look back at' from the sentence after, for that matter).

Read the following analysis of 'Love Songs in Age' by Philip Larkin and, as you read, think about what verbs you would use to replace the highlighted phrasal verbs:

> Larkin's exploration of nostalgia is evoked powerfully in the simile 'the unfailing sense of being young/Spread out like a spring-woken tree'. The adjective 'unfailing' indicates how pleasant memories of the past stick in our minds and can crop up when summoned. The compound adjective 'spring-woken' illustrates how, like nature awakening after winter, past events can come back to us unexpectedly when prompted by a stimulus from our youth. Through this image, Larkin portrays the speaker's futile desire to go back to a golden period of her life.

How did you get on? Hopefully you will have thought of some verbs that are a) more formal, b) more succinct, and c) more impressive sounding. Here's what a different student came up with:

> Larkin's exploration of nostalgia is evoked powerfully in the simile 'the unfailing sense of being young/Spread out like a spring-woken tree'. The adjective 'unfailing' indicates how pleasant memories of the past persist and can revive when summoned. The compound adjective 'spring-woken' illustrates how, like nature awakening after winter, past events can intrude unexpectedly when prompted by a stimulus from our youth. Through this image, Larkin portrays the speaker's futile desire to revisit a golden period of her life.

6. Cut out wasteful words

As well as ditching clunky phrasal verbs, there are other ways to declare war on waffle in your writing. When you're revising for difficult exams where time is at a premium, the last thing you want to do is use unnecessary words and phrases:

> A large proportion of Seamus Heaney's poems deal with the idea of youthful innocence. 'Out of the Bag' is one such poem, using a man by the name of Dr Kerlin to lift the lid on the esoteric secret of childbirth. The title itself gives a strong sense of the ways in which we can view the beginning of life. A popular idiom, 'out of the bag' is ambiguous, as it can refer to letting everyone in on a secret. Alternatively, it can refer to Dr Kerlin's 'bag' of mysterious medical instruments. In the case of Heaney's poem, it cannot be denied that the perspective encourages the reader to share the speaker's naïve appreciation with regard to the wonders of our arrival into this world.

Now see how by hacking away at the overgrowth of waffle, we can write with much more clarity and brevity:

> Many of Seamus Heaney's poems address themes of youthful innocence. 'Out of the Bag' is one such poem, using the character Dr Kerlin to divulge the esoteric secret of childbirth. The title explores how we can view life's origins. A popular idiom, 'out of the bag' is ambiguous, as it can refer to revealing a secret. Alternatively, it suggests Dr Kerlin's 'bag' of mysterious medical instruments. With Heaney's poem, the perspective undeniably aligns the reader to the speaker's naïve appreciation of the wonders of our birth.

The improved example may not be perfect but it's much better than the first draft. Work on your own paragraphs in this way and you'll find your word counts plummet as your readability improves.

7. Be clear and concise

In addition to cutting out waffle, there are other prominent issues that stop students writing well at A-level.

Students often lose themselves in the flow of their thought and end up writing very long, one-sentence paragraphs. Grammatically incorrect sentences like in the following example tend to display very muddled thinking and the ideas become difficult to understand:

> Although it's a comic play, *Twelfth Night* contains moments of
> wistful melancholy, for example when the clownlike Sir Andrew
> Aguecheek laments that he 'was adored once too', which gives
> the impression, through the past tense adverb 'once', which
> implies that this was firstly in the past and secondly something
> that occurred on just a single occasion, in addition the use of
> the emotive verb 'adored' implies that it was a deep and lasting
> relationship, making the end of it and the passing of time all
> the more poignant and for this reason despite all the moments
> of light relief we are still left with a sense of the transient nature
> of romantic love and the lasting impression it can leave on those
> that have lost it.

Paragraphs like this become increasingly incomprehensible to an examiner. Try reading it aloud and see how exhausting it is: a jumble of potentially interesting ideas ruined by a lack of punctuation and control. You might not think that you'd ever write like this in an exam but, under pressure, plenty of students do. So use the time you have during revision to practise crafting elegant sentences and memorising the key parts of your analysis to use and adapt to different essay questions. Students can fall into the trap of trying to ensure that every single word they use is complex, which also leaves their ideas very tricky to work out. To overcome this, practise using impressive vocabulary carefully, making sure its use is necessary and the meaning of your sentences remains clear.

8. Make use of nominalisation

Nominalisation is a key feature of effective academic writing. It sounds very complicated but, with a bit of practice, it's much easier than you think. Formal written English uses nouns more than verbs. This process of changing a verb or another word into a noun is called nominalisation. For example, 'satisfaction' rather than 'satisfy', 'entertainment' instead of 'entertain'.

Let's take a look at what this might look like, with a before-and-after nominalisation example.

Before:

> By comparing Desdemona to a 'pearl', Shakespeare shows Othello
> is acknowledging that her whiteness allowed him to become
> more accepted by the Venetian state. The simile also portrays
> Desdemona as entrapped by this same patriarchal society, like a
> 'pearl' without its shell, depicting her as weak and vulnerable.

After:

By comparing Desdemona to a 'pearl', Shakespeare shows Othello's acknowledgment of her whiteness in allowing him to gain greater acceptance by the Venetian state. The simile also portrays Desdemona's entrapment by this same patriarchal society; like a 'pearl' without its shell, her depiction implies weakness and vulnerability.

9. Include appositives

Like nominalisation, using appositives is a key ingredient of successful academic writing. Appositives are nouns or noun phrases that rename another noun right beside it. They are used to identify, explain or provide extra information about that word. They might use just a few words or a longer phrase. Here are just a few examples of how this small grammatical feature can really add sophistication to your sentences:

- **A cold and aggressive character,** Tom Buchanan is memorably described as a 'brute of a man'.
- **A poet who spent his childhood immersed in books and daydreams,** Coleridge viewed his education as a process of separation from his family and nature.
- Increasingly deranged, Victor Frankenstein pursues the creature to the Arctic Circle, **one of several undomesticated Gothic landscapes that appear in the novel**.
- Claudius, **a devious and ambitious character driven by lust,** recognises his moral degradation by talking of his 'rank' conduct.
- Terry Eagleton, **a renowned critic who approaches the text through a Marxist lens,** argues that in order to gain revenge on the society that manipulated him, Heathcliff must join that very system and become 'a pitiless capitalist landlord'.

10. Vary sentences with participle phrases

Participle phrases are another key feature of excellent academic writing. They can be roughly split into two categories: present participle phrases and past participle phrases. If it's a present participle phrase, the participle will end in '-ing'. If it's a past participle phrase, the participle will usually end in '-ed' (some verbs are irregular and don't fit this pattern). Look at the following examples.

Present participles:

- **Pronouncing that the character is 'heroically sound in the goodness of his heart',** Harold Bloom contends that Bottom is 'a triumphant early instance of Shakespeare's invention of the human'.

- **Describing his fellow refugees through the zoomorphic noun 'swarms',** Daljit Nagra's speaker appropriates, and simultaneously ridicules, xenophobic attitudes towards British identity.

- Dystopian texts dealing with ecological disaster are increasingly commonplace. J.G. Ballard, **writing as far back as the 1960s,** created a setting where great swathes of North America and Europe are placed under water, **depicting apocalyptic conditions where only reptiles can thrive.**

Past participles:

- **Obliterated by an unexpected tempest,** the Turkish invasion of Cyprus is over before 'fair warrior' Othello has set foot on the island.

- **Exposed to the chaotic nature of public life, portrayed as 'being out, out, far out to sea and alone',** Mrs Dalloway appears metaphorically adrift in the urban jungle of London.

- **Driven mad by her inculcation at the red centre,** the impact of Janine's accumulated trauma is evoked through the simile 'like a puppy that's been kicked too often'.

Practising the use of participles and appositives, scheduled in as an important part of your revision, will ensure that highly effective sentence structures become an integral feature of your writing.

66 Top 5 to thrive

1. Address all key words from questions throughout your essay.

2. Focus on analysing characters and use hedging language if in doubt.

3. Cut out colloquial and unnecessary language, and use punctuation carefully to control sentence length.

4. Practise nominalising verbs to make your writing sound more academic.

5. Incorporate appositives and participle phrases to add further sophistication to your essays.

Improving practice essays

You've learnt the quotes. You've selected the ones you think are the most significant. You know what context fits best with which bits of analysis. You've practised writing paragraphs in class, and as part of your revision.

By now you're ready to tackle practice essay questions. Before you start writing these essays during revision, let's quickly remind ourselves of the ingredients of a good A-level English Literature essay:

- An effective introduction (thesis statement)
- Main body – includes analysis of writer's methods
- Exploration of context and critical interpretations (where applicable)
- A logical structure that answers the question
- Clear comparison (where necessary)
- A neat conclusion
- Well-written, with interesting ideas

In my experience, students understand why they need to practise writing responses to essay questions. Just like in Maths or Geography or Spanish, they know that having a go at previous exam questions will help them prepare for future ones. They struggle, however, with knowing how to revise for English essays. They know roughly what needs to go into an English essay. But they don't always know precisely how to practise these key ingredients.

So how can I revise these parts of an essay?

Before we look at the separate sections of an essay, there's one important thing I want to tell you about essays, revision and exams.

Students who do well in exams usually have a very clear idea about what they're going to write before they go into the exam!

This means they'll have done lots of practice writing parts of essays in revision. They'll have practised putting the best paragraphs together to form impressive full essays. They'll have practised tweaking these essays to fit other similar exam questions. And, most crucially, they'll have used retrieval practice to memorise the best chunks of their work.

One I made earlier – how to prepare quality essay responses

✓ Write practice paragraphs on your key quotes.

✓ Improve them during revision.

✓ Use your introduction as an essay plan.

✓ Practise getting your best paragraphs into essays.

✓ Spend time adapting these essays to fit other exam questions.

✓ Memorise the best parts of your essays.

Preparing essay introductions for novels and plays

Why are introductions such an important part of your revision? I usually find that students who struggle to write an effective introduction haven't planned out what they are going to write about. For this reason, their introductions are usually full of waffle.

At A-level, teachers tend to refer to introductions as thesis statements. A good thesis statement will, in a few sentences, frame your overall response to the question. It will introduce the main points of your argument and will address some of the key ideas of the text.

The best introductions make complex points in a few sentences. They understand that writers create characters, not real people. They understand the key ideas and the bigger picture. They know what the writer was trying to say when they wrote the text.

Here's an example for a question about the theme of madness in *Hamlet*:

> Hamlet's madness is initially a 'craft[ed]' mechanism that facilitates his manipulation of other characters. Yet, by the play's denouement, Hamlet's 'antic disposition' has propelled him to genuine insanity. In foregrounding Hamlet's obsession with truth – 'that one may smile...and be a villain' – Shakespeare emphasises how a deep understanding of mankind's capacity for evil can lead to tragic mental disintegration.

This example gets across the following key ideas:

- Hamlet feigns madness to gain power.
- In faking madness, he becomes mad.
- Hamlet is motivated by a quest to get to the truth.
- A greater awareness of our capacity for evil can lead to insanity.

This introduction can now be used as an outline plan for the rest of the essay. By matching these key ideas with your favourite quotes on the theme of madness, you can logically move through the main body of your essay, making sure you properly answer the question.

What about other essay questions?

An important part of your revision is practising adapting the introduction for similar theme questions. For *Hamlet*, this might include:

- Appearance versus reality
- The position of women
- Action and inaction
- Corruption
- Death and decay

For example:

> Hamlet's madness is initially a 'craft[ed]' *disguise, an appearance* that facilitates his manipulation of other characters. Yet, by the play's denouement, Hamlet's 'antic disposition' has *become reality, propelling* him to genuine insanity. In foregrounding Hamlet's obsession with truth – 'that one may smile...and be a villain' – Shakespeare *exposes* how *lifting the veil* of mankind's capacity for evil can lead to tragic mental disintegration.

Let's take a look at another example, this time a question with a character focus, from *Hard Times*:

> Portrayed as a mechanical and unemotional character at the start of the novel, Mr Gradgrind's views of children as 'reasoning animal[s]' represent the cold Utilitarian philosophy of Victorian Britain. In caricaturing Gradgrind's desire to 'plant nothing else [but] facts', Dickens critiques the hard-headed ideology of nineteenth century industrialists who proposed that children should be devoid of emotion. At the end of the novel, however, Gradgrind's moral transformation is used to symbolise the redemptive power of human relationships, and act as a reminder to society that although 'there is a wisdom of the Head', far more vital is 'a wisdom of the Heart'.

This example gets across the following key ideas about Thomas Gradgrind:

- At the start, he symbolises the coldness of Utilitarianism philosophy.
- Dickens uses his character to question ideas about industrial mechanization.
- Gradgrind undergoes a significant change in the novel.
- His relationship with his children convinces him of the importance of human emotion.

As with the *Hamlet* example, this introduction can act as a plan for the rest of the essay's paragraphs.

Notice how all of the examples I've given focus on the key words ('appearance versus reality', for example) from the questions in the introduction. As well as referring to it at the start, examiners will expect you to refer to the key word from the question throughout the full essay. When using my method of adapting prepared responses, it's really important that you do this, or you will lose marks!

Preparing essay introductions for poetry

An excellent way of showing you understand the main techniques and ideas in the poems is to prepare a brief thesis statement for each of the poems from the collections that you study. I recommend that my students use this format:

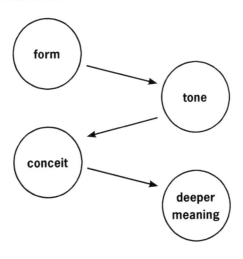

What do these terms mean?

Form is the type of poem. For example, an elegy is a type of poem written to remember someone who has died. A sonnet is a 14-line poem, traditionally written in iambic pentameter. A didactic poem instructs the reader and gives a clear moral message.

Tone is the writer's or speaker's attitude towards a subject. This is revealed through their point of view or choice of words.

Conceit is an inventive or original idea, in the form of an extended metaphor that runs throughout the poem.

Deeper meaning is the poem's key ideas or themes. This is often hidden beneath the surface meaning of the poem.

'A Minor Role' by U.A. Fanthorpe

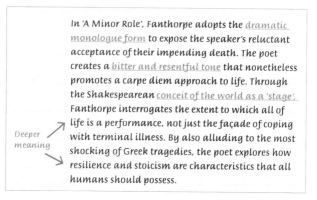

In 'A Minor Role', Fanthorpe adopts the _dramatic monologue form_ to expose the speaker's reluctant acceptance of their impending death. The poet creates a _bitter and resentful tone_ that nonetheless promotes a carpe diem approach to life. Through the Shakespearean _conceit of the world as a 'stage'_, Fanthorpe interrogates the extent to which all of life is a performance, not just the façade of coping with terminal illness. By also alluding to the most shocking of Greek tragedies, the poet explores how resilience and stoicism are characteristics that all humans should possess.

Deeper meaning

Using this structure, you can plan introductions for all of the poems that you study. A key focus for A-level revision is planning for the comparison questions that are part of your poetry exam. Depending on the exam board and specification that you are doing, you will be asked to compare the named poem with either prose, drama, unseen poems or other poems from your anthology. During revision, you can practise including comparison in these introductions by bringing in a second text. The following example compares an anthology poem with an unseen poem:

Comparing 'A Minor Role' to an unseen poem called 'Differences of Opinion' by Wendy Cope

> By contrast, in 'Differences of Opinion', Cope uses the lyric form to explore how men can silence female viewpoints. Both speakers adopt a tone of resigned acceptance towards their assigned role in life. Yet this is conveyed in a different way: in 'A Minor Role' illness shapes the speaker's lack of agency, whereas in 'Differences of Opinion' the speaker sarcastically ridicules how patriarchal structures encourage men to 'stand their ground'.
>
> Deeper meaning → Through the conceit of the woman losing an argument despite 'him' being logically defeated, Cope exposes how patronising sophistry doesn't hinder men's celebration of 'flat earth' ideas. Like in 'A Minor Role', the speaker has to unwillingly submit to a more powerful force in their life.

Preparing the main body of your essay

Here's an example question for the novel *The Handmaid's Tale* by Margaret Atwood:

How does Atwood explore ideas about memory in *The Handmaid's Tale*?

As part of their revision, a student has written a practice paragraph, using one of the killer quotes from Chapter 3:

> Atwood has asserted that as a writer she is 'more interested in social history than in the biographies of the outstanding'. A clear example of the focus on the individual memory in society can be found in Offred's recollection 'I used to think of my body as an instrument, of pleasure...Now the flesh arranges itself differently. I'm a cloud, congealed around a central object'.
>
> Offred's 'body' was once the manifestation of her free will, capable of feeling passion and excitement, evoking nostalgic memories of freedom and choice. Yet the chremamorphism of 'cloud' repositions Offred's physical self as something nebulous and intangible. In euphemising her reproductive organs as Offred's 'central object', Atwood shows how Offred has internalised the state's dehumanisation of her, which, at this stage of the novel, reduces her to victim rather than 'outstanding' heroine status.

This is an impressive paragraph. It includes:

- Relevant context, linked to the question.
- Close analysis of language, linked back to the context.
- Ambitious vocabulary and sophisticated terminology.
- An evaluation of the writer's intentions.

So, now the student needs to (a) memorise sections of the paragraph and (b) practise tweaking it for similar exam questions.

For example, could the student fit this paragraph into a question where, instead of memory, the key theme is:

- Individuals and the state?
- Freedom?
- Loss of identity?
- Misuse of power?
- Gender conflict?
- Sexual reproduction?
- The past and the present?

Yes! After a bit of thought and practice the student has easily recycled this paragraph for the question on loss of identity:

> Atwood has asserted that as a writer she is 'more interested in social history than in the biographies of the outstanding'. A clear example of how character memories reveal a loss of personal identity can be found in Offred's recollection 'I used to think of my body as an instrument, of pleasure...Now the flesh arranges itself differently. I'm a cloud, congealed around a central object'.
>
> Offred's 'body', a fundamental part of identity, was once the manifestation of her free will, capable of feeling passion and excitement, evoking nostalgic memories of freedom and choice. Yet the chremamorphism of 'cloud' repositions Offred's physical self as something nebulous and intangible. In euphemising her reproductive organs as Offred's 'central object', Atwood shows how Offred has internalised the state's assault on her self-identity. As such, she is portrayed as the antithesis of an 'outstanding' heroine.

Now let's look at an example from *Dracula*:

How does Stoker explore ideas about sex and seduction in *Dracula*?

> Through his construction of Lucy's transformation from demure innocence to a character who becomes 'cold-blooded' and 'wanton', Stoker examines attitudes towards female sexual promiscuity in conservative Victorian society. The scene depicting the destruction of Lucy's demon uses sexualised imagery to highlight contemporary fears about feminine desire. The 'hardened' stake is undoubtedly phallic in nature, and it is noteworthy that Stoker ensures that Arthur drives the penis symbol 'deeper and deeper...through' Lucy. The diacopic repetition of the comparative 'deeper' indicates a perceived necessary forcefulness to the symbolically sexual act. As a result of Arthur's reassertion of his penetrative control over Lucy – ironically returning her to a state of monogamous virtue – nineteenth century male readers witness a reassuring removal of the sexual threat posed by female insatiability.

Next, the student has thought about how this paragraph might fit a question with a similar focus:

- Death and the undead
- Illness and decay
- Madness
- Modernity
- Relationships and romance
- Fear of the outsider
- Christianity and the occult
- The human body

As a result, the sex and seduction paragraph has been reworked to fit the human body question:

> The transformation of Lucy's bodily appetites reflects her transition from demure innocence to a character who becomes 'cold-blooded' and 'wanton'. Through this portrayal, Stoker examines attitudes towards female sexual promiscuity in conservative Victorian society. The scene depicting the removal of Lucy's demon through the destruction of her heart uses sexualised imagery to highlight contemporary fears about feminine desire. The 'hardened' stake is undoubtedly phallic in nature, and it is noteworthy that Stoker ensures that Arthur drives the penis symbol 'deeper and deeper...through' Lucy. The diacopic repetition of the comparative 'deeper' indicates a perceived necessary forcefulness to the symbolically sexual act.

As a result of Arthur's reassertion of his penetrative control over Lucy's body – ironically returning her to a state of monogamous virtue – nineteenth century male readers witness a reassuring removal of the sexual threat posed by physical manifestations of female insatiability.

What if my prepared essay paragraphs don't fit the question?

Sometimes, you will read a question and panic. We didn't study this theme! My quotes and planned paragraphs won't fit! This is a nightmare! I've been there.

I've sat in English exams and had a minute of anxiety and perspiration. Fortunately, I composed myself and remembered my teacher's wise words: *questions are there to be taken on. If you don't like the wording of a question, flip it on its head.*

For example, questions about power can also focus on characters that are powerless and vulnerable. Or we can carefully consider wider meanings of the key word.

So, a question about 'appearance and reality' can focus on:

- the difference between the human world and the fantasy world
- what characters seem to be like and how they behave in reality
- truth and deception
- the façade versus inner feelings
- confusion and madness caused by uncertainty about what is real and what is not.

This gives you much more to write about than just thinking about one narrow idea or theme.

Here's another example of how you might re-frame a typical A-level English Literature question:

How does _____ present conflict in _____?

Depending on which text you're studying, conflict could refer to:

- Physical violence
- Psychological confusion
- Inner conflict
- Appearance versus reality

- Past versus present
- Binary opposites
- Prejudice/oppression
- Man versus nature
- Dreams versus reality

Looking at questions in this way gives you a much greater chance of being able to use your planned essay. But to be on the safe side, it's an excellent idea to build up a bank of prepared essays.

A student studying *Atonement*, for example, might have three ready-to-go essays that cover the following theme questions:

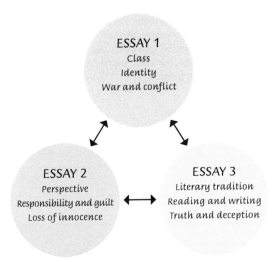

ESSAY 1
Class
Identity
War and conflict

ESSAY 2
Perspective
Responsibility and guilt
Loss of innocence

ESSAY 3
Literary tradition
Reading and writing
Truth and deception

As the diagram suggests, the student has noticed that there are links between some of these themes. This means they should be able to 'borrow' paragraphs from the essays, depending on the type of extract or exact wording of the question.

Conclusions

In English exams, time passes quickly. You don't get the time to write a detailed conclusion. For this reason, many students don't bother. They analyse right up until the clock, often finishing mid-sentence.

The main body of your essay is the most important part. It will form the bulk of your marks. But a neat, concise conclusion can beautifully sum up your opinion of the question.

I get my students to make a couple of quick points at the end of their essay:

1. Refer back to the key word in the question, summing up your ideas about the importance of that theme or character in the text.

2. Explain, once more, the author's intention. What message were they trying to give about society?

Take a look at this example conclusion for a *Mrs Dalloway* question:

How does Woolf explore ideas about female identity?

1 — Woolf's portrayal of Clarissa recognises the fundamental importance of a rich inner life, elevating it to the 'most precious possession', which is fundamental to the expression of authentic female identity.

2 — Far from just allowing the opportunity for introspection, for Woolf, the inner life is a vital sanctuary, offering the chance for women to escape the anxieties of modernity and find genuine spiritual freedom.

Can I plan these in advance as well?

Of course. As with the introductions and main paragraphs, conclusions can be crafted before the day and adapted to fit different questions. Get these nailed down and memorised and you'll soon be nearing the end of your essay writing revision!

66 Top 5 to thrive

1. Make sure your essays include the key ingredients.

2. Prepare high-quality practice paragraphs and full essays in advance.

3. Plan introductions, main body paragraphs and conclusions, using my structures and examples if you're stuck.

4. Think carefully about which questions are similar to each other, as this can allow you to use a similar response.

5. Try to widen the meaning of the question so you can play to your strengths.

99

Getting ready for the unseen texts

Students often worry about starting revision for English Literature. But, from having studied the subject at GCSE, at least they have a solid understanding of most of the things they need to do: know the plot; understand the characters and themes; memorise relevant context and critical quotes.

Yet, when it comes to unseen texts many students feel really concerned. They don't know where to begin. I've seen very confident students tremble at the prospect of preparing for a section of the exam on something they've *never studied before*!

There's no need for you to feel anxious about the unseen questions. There are things that you can do to help you feel more prepared for unseen texts. I'm going to share a few tricks that I think will leave you feeling ready to tackle anything that's thrown at you.

What unseen sections do I need to plan for?

Unseen poetry

Most of the exam boards ask students to study unseen poetry. If your school or college does OCR for A-level English Literature, you won't need to study unseen poetry, so OCR students can now skip to the unseen prose section. For those studying other exam boards, here's what you'll be expected to do for the unseen poetry question:

Exam board	Will I study unseen poetry?	What will I need to compare this with?
Edexcel	Yes (post-2000 poem)	Choice of two named poems from post-2000 anthology
AQA	Yes (from any era)	Compare the two unseen poems that you are given
Eduqas	Yes (from any era)	No comparison required
OCR	No	

How can I prepare for unseen poetry?

Tackling poems that you haven't studied before can seem intimidating. Many students find unseen poetry difficult. At A-level, they often find the concepts more challenging and the language harder to decipher. They can struggle with the abstract ideas. They sometimes fail to spot the less obvious themes.

As with all other revision, however, practice is vital. The more unseen poems you look at, the more confident you will feel about the exam, especially if you have a routine that helps you look for clues. Here's the step-by-step guide I suggest to my students:

A step-by-step guide to unseen poems

✔ Read the poem at least twice

✔ Titles are important

✔ So are final lines

✔ Devices/techniques matter

✔ But the effect is most important

✔ Link effect to deeper themes/symbolism

✔ Structure – where's the volta?

✔ If in doubt, use hedging language

To begin with, **read the poem carefully** without making any annotations. Try not to jump to any conclusions about the poem's meaning on this first reading. Read the question, as this should give you a clue about the poem's key themes. On the second reading, pick out interesting words, devices or structure. Don't attempt to do a line-by-line summary or 'translation' of the poem. Pick out four or five parts that grab your attention. Make sure these are linked to the question.

Poets think long and hard about **the title** they use for a poem. Look at it carefully. It should give you an indication about the main ideas behind the poem.

The same goes for **final lines**. These often act as a conclusion that summarises the main idea of the poem. Good final lines are usually thought-provoking and can surprise the reader.

Poems generally make use of figurative language and other interesting **poetic devices** such as metre, caesura and enjambment. Knowing these techniques can really help your understanding of the poet's intentions, BUT...

Being able to spot different literary devices is useless without a **clear explanation of their effect**. The most important part of your analysis is explaining the impact of the writer's choices.

Once you've read the poem a few times and thought about the poet's methods, you can start to consider the possible meaning of the poem. Start off with some obvious questions. What happens in the poem? What are the speaker's feelings? What does it seem to be about? Then you can dig beneath the surface and **look for deeper meaning**: what is it really about?

Students often forget to write about the structure of the poem. Or they make vague comments about how the poem looks on the page, which doesn't pick up good marks. A more sophisticated way to write about structure is to **focus on the volta**. The volta (Italian for 'turn') is the part found in many poems, often signalled by words such as 'but' or 'yet', where there is a distinct change of tone. Looking at this section of a poem can help you understand shifts in mood or perspective.

If you're struggling to reach a definitive interpretation of a poem, it's better to be cautious than trying to sound definite and possibly getting it badly wrong. If in doubt, use **hedging language** (words and phrases like 'perhaps', 'possibly', 'could be argued') to be on the safe side.

Putting it into practice

Let's have a look at a practice unseen poetry question:

Explore how the poet places a value on love in 'Love is Not All'.

Love is Not All

Love is not all: it is not meat nor drink
Nor slumber nor a roof against the rain;
Nor yet a floating spar to men that sink
And rise and sink and rise and sink again;
Love can not fill the thickened lung with breath,
Nor clean the blood, nor set the fractured bone;
Yet many a man is making friends with death
Even as I speak, for lack of love alone.
It well may be that in a difficult hour,
Pinned down by pain and moaning for release,
Or nagged by want past resolution's power,
I might be driven to sell your love for peace,
Or trade the memory of this night for food.
It well may be. I do not think I would.

Edna St. Vincent Millay

- **Reading the poem twice** should help you notice things like the zoomorphic image of the human as a trapped and wounded animal, 'pinned down by pain and moaning for release'. This image contributes to the motif of survival, suggested by mundane concrete nouns and noun phrases such as 'food', 'meat', 'drink', 'floating spar', and 'roof against the rain'. Through this juxtaposition between essential or life-saving items and the less tangible concept of love, is the speaker questioning its real value to an individual?

- On the surface, **the title** 'Love is Not All' offers a definitive opinion that downplays the significance of love. Through the negative adverb 'not', Millay's speaker appears to utterly reject love's seemingly universal power. And yet the certainty of the title contrasts with the latter part of the poem. Dig deeper and we find a greater deal of ambiguity than first suspected: love is later revealed to be not sufficient in itself but still very necessary.

- The poetic voice is less certain but more optimistic in **the final lines**. They 'may' swap their memories of love for life's basic needs. But they feel reasonably confident that they wouldn't. This final line subverts the hyperbole of traditional love poetry; gone are the exaggerated vows to die for one's love. As the disharmony of the half-rhyming final couplet implies, this speaker is more hesitant and realistic: love is important, but they can't promise they'd be willing to sacrifice their life for it!

- Some interesting **poetic devices**: the diacopic repetition of 'sink' indicates our desperate need to be rescued from the currents, both literal and metaphorical, when the force of nature intervenes. 'Love' is personified but displays relative weakness in not being able to 'fill the thickened lung with breath'. As a result, at this stage of the poem love is portrayed as lacking the magical qualities it is frequently given in the Petrarchan tradition, which is ironic as the poet has adopted the sonnet form and iambic pentameter associated with romance poetry.

- The grotesque imagery of the 'thickened lung' has a powerful **effect on the reader**. When followed by the line 'nor clean the blood', it amplifies the sense of love's inability to overcome decay and disease of the body (possibly tuberculosis in this case). Love may have value, but in the face of human mortality it is presented as impotent.

- The poem begins with the idea that love is comparatively insignificant as it cannot sustain human life and cannot heal our damaged bodies. Yet, as the poem concludes, we see **the deeper meaning**. Despite using a rational and objective voice to list love's inadequacies, the speaker admits at the end that, nonetheless, they might also be susceptible to valuing love above life's more pragmatic concerns.

- There is a significant shift in tone with **the volta**: 'Yet many a man is making friends with death/Even as I speak, for lack of love alone'. Before the volta, love is ineffectual and inconsequential. After this structural shift, we discover that, despite being impractical it can encourage men to risk their lives for it. In ending with the optimistic phrase 'I would', the poet perhaps indicates that, despite the speaker's initial reservations, love has even more power than seemingly more critical essentials.

- Look at my example of **hedging language** in the last sentence above. My use of 'perhaps' and 'seemingly' shows that I'm not absolutely certain about this interpretation. It's an interesting idea but it might be a leap too far, so I'm being cautious with my language.

Use this approach with all the practice unseen questions that you do in class and during revision.

What about introductions?

Remember the approach that I showed you to poetry introductions in the last chapter? Well, this method can also be used for unseen poetry:

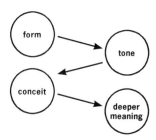

Applying this model to 'Love is Not All':

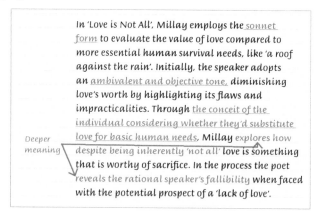

What about comparing an unseen poem with another poem?

As with the anthology poems that we began comparing in the last chapter, you can also practise incorporating comparison in these introductions by bringing in a second poem. The following example does this with another unseen poem – 'A Winter's Tale' by D.H. Lawrence:

A Winter's Tale

Yesterday the fields were only grey with scattered snow,
And now the longest grass-leaves hardly emerge;
Yet her deep footsteps mark the snow, and go
On towards the pines at the hills' white verge.

I cannot see her, since the mist's white scarf
Obscures the dark wood and the dull orange sky;
But she's waiting, I know, impatient and cold, half
Sobs struggling into her frosty sigh.

Why does she come so promptly, when she must know
That she's only the nearer to the inevitable farewell;
The hill is steep, on the snow my steps are slow –
Why does she come, when she knows what I have to tell?

D.H. Lawrence

By contrast, in 'A Winter's Tale', Lawrence uses the
pastoral form to depict love as a phenomenon that
necessarily involves an 'inevitable farewell'. Like the
speaker in 'Love is Not All', the voice in 'A Winter's
Tale' also conveys an ambivalent attitude towards
the popular conception of love as an eternal and
all-conquering force. Yet, unlike Millay, Lawrence
creates a melancholic tone to illustrate the
speaker's feelings of regret at having to terminate
a relationship that is clearly valued highly by the
'sob[bing]' girl. Through the conceit of the rural idyll
covered in frost, Lawrence highlights the speaker's
reluctance to 'tell' the truth about the death of
love. As with Millay's speaker, however, Lawrence's
speaker may perhaps also be less certain of their
'obscure[d]' perceptions about love than they first
appear. The symbolic reference to the 'deep footsteps'

*Deeper
meaning* — implies that, like in 'Love is Not All', love is capable
of leaving a more lasting impression on rational
individuals than they care to acknowledge.

How can I prepare for unseen prose extracts?

Most of the exam boards also require you to analyse an unseen extract. Again, as the table below shows, there are variations across exam boards about how you are expected to approach this. If you are doing the Edexcel papers, you don't need to do unseen prose, so you can skip this section.

Exam board	Will I study unseen prose?	What will I need to compare this with?
Edexcel	No	
AQA (Specification A)	Yes (from WWI onwards)	Compare with one drama and one prose text you've studied
AQA (Specification B)	Yes (from 1945 onwards)	Compare with one drama and one prose text you've studied
Eduqas	Yes (choice of two extracts from different time periods)	No comparison required but you need to reference the short supporting extracts
OCR	Yes (from the genre or era of literature that you study)	Compare with two prose texts you've studied

Putting it into practice

Let's have a look at a practice extract, from Chapter 14 of the novel *So Big* (1924) by Edna Ferber. This section tells the story of a young man called Dirk De Jong, who has left his home in a poor Dutch farming community on the edge of Chicago and has gone away to university:

Throughout Dirk's Freshman year there were, for him, no heartening, informal, mellow talks before the wood-fire in the book-lined study of some professor whose wisdom was such a mixture of classic lore and modernism as to be an inspiration to his listeners. Midwest professors delivered their lectures in the classroom as they had been delivering them in the past ten or twenty years and as they would deliver them until death or a trustees' meeting should remove them. The younger professors and instructors in natty grey suits and bright-coloured ties made a point of being unpedantic in the classroom and rather overdid it. They posed as being one of the fellows; would dashingly use a bit of slang to create a laugh from the boys and an adoring titter from the girls. Dirk somehow preferred the pedants to these. When these had to give an informal talk to the men before some university event they would start by saying, "Now listen, fellahs—". At the dances they were not above "rushing" the pretty co-eds.

Two of Dirk's classes were conducted by women professors. They were well on toward middle age, or past it; desiccated women. Only their eyes were alive. Their clothes were of some indefinite dark stuff, brown or drab-grey; their hair lifeless; their hands long, bony, unvital. They had seen classes and classes and classes. A roomful of fresh young faces that appeared briefly only to be replaced by another roomful of fresh young faces like round white pencil marks manipulated momentarily on a slate, only to be sponged off to give way to other round white marks. Of the two women one — the elder — was occasionally likely to flare into sudden life; a flame in the ashes of a burned-out grate. She had humour and a certain caustic wit, qualities that had managed miraculously to survive even the deadly and numbing effects of thirty years in the classroom. A fine mind, and iconoclastic, hampered by the restrictions of a conventional community and the soul of a congenital spinster.

Under the guidance of these Dirk chafed and grew restless. Miss Euphemia Hollingswood had a way of emphasising every third or fifth syllable, bringing her voice down hard on it, thus:

"In the *consideration of all* the facts in the *case* presented *before* us we must *first* review the *history* and *attempt* to analyse the *outstanding*—"

He found himself waiting for that emphasis and shrinking from it as from a sledge-hammer blow. It hurt his head.

Miss Lodge droned. She approached a word with a maddening uh-uh-uh-uh. In the uh-uh-uh face of the uh-uh-uh-uh geometrical situation of the uh-uh-uh uh…

He shifted restlessly in his chair, found his hands clenched into fists, and took refuge in watching the shadow cast by an oak branch outside the window on a patch of sunlight against the blackboard behind her.

Language: example exploded quote

The grotesque adjective 'desiccated' implies extreme dryness. From the judgemental perspective of a teenager, the women are depicted as shrivelled and unappealing. A Freudian interpretation of this harsh viewpoint might question whether a young man who has left his mother for the first time might be unconsciously revealing his disgust at the lack of sexual appeal of similar aged females.

'They were well on toward middle age, or past it; desiccated women. Only their eyes were alive...their hands long, bony, unvital.'

The clichéd idiom dictates that "the eyes are the window to the soul". Perhaps in personifying these body parts, the author intends to foreshadow a deeper, more perceptive side to Dirk's character. Beyond the misogynistic harshness, there is a glimmer of recognition that, beyond shallow appraisals of their bodies, these women have intelligence and vivacity at their core.

On the surface, Ferber appears to use this description to encourage the reader to distance themselves further from Dirk's sexist scrutiny of his female lecturers. The tripartite pattern almost caricatures the women as witches, complete with near skeletal hands. Yet, when juxtaposed with the observation 'deadly and numbing effects of thirty years in the classroom', it appears that on further inspection the writer is perhaps hyperbolising the restless undergrad's feelings of sympathy for his bored professors.

Structure: example analysis

At the beginning of the extract, Ferber focuses our attention on Dirk's fantasy vision of congenial and welcoming discussions with his teachers: 'mellow talks before the wood-fire in the book-lined study of some professor'. The 'wood-fire' evokes images of the light, warmth and domesticity that signals to the reader Dirk's subconscious yearning for the home he has recently left. The unspecified determiner 'some' indicates that Dirk's needs are universal. As a young man adrift at college, he craves any kind of scholarly hospitality.

By the end of the extract, Ferber has revisited the motif of comforting light, with the description, 'took refuge in watching the shadow cast by an oak branch outside the window on a patch of sunlight'. This circular narrative helps the reader to recognise Dirk's growing alienation with his tedious academic surroundings, particularly when juxtaposed with the bucolic scene of a tree in the sunshine. It's almost as if the 'branch' is personified and is reaching out to offer the welcome the university will not. The contrast between the tone of disillusionment at the opening and the final tone of profound cynicism provokes feelings of pathos from the reader. As a result of this significant structural shift, we are left feeling concerned that the ominous 'clenched fists' of frustration may symbolise the death of Dirk's academic dream and instead foreshadow a descent into violence.

Use this approach as part of your revision with each practice paper you attempt. The more papers you do at home, the more you will get the hang of picking out the important ideas and themes.

How can I practise comparing unseen texts?

If you are taking exams by a board that expects you to compare unseen poetry or unseen prose with other texts, you'll need to practise planning the comparisons that will make up the main body of your essays. Here's an example, using the two unseen poems from earlier in the chapter, that shows how you can practise quick plans as part of your revision:

Comparing writers' methods: example plan

'Love is Not All'

- Objective tone exposes the inessential and impractical nature of love:

'Love can not fill the thickened lung with breath'

- Uses euphemism to gently allude to love's power and how men will sacrifice their lives for love:

'making friends with death'

- Final line uses modal verb to imply probability that rational speaker is also fallible to love's influence:

'I do not think I would'

'A Winter's Tale'

- **Also** recognises love's limitations but **unlike** Millay's speaker adopts a melancholic and bewildered tone:

'nearer to the inevitable farewell'

- **By contrast**, uses metaphor to allude to the speaker's unconscious realisation that love will leave a powerful lasting impression:

'deep footsteps'

- Whereas Lawrence uses lexical verb in final line to convey a **different** attitude to love: poet asserts that we have to recognise that love can be destructive as well as redemptive:

'what I have to tell'

66 Top 5 to thrive

1. Check which parts of your A-level English Literature exams feature unseen texts.

2. Follow a step-by-step guide to each unseen poem you attempt.

3. For unseen poetry introductions, use my four-stage model.

4. Practise a variety of unseen prose extracts, focusing on language, structure and writer's intention.

5. For the relevant unseen sections of your exams, practise comparing writers' methods.

99

Taking care of yourself and coping with exams

To perform well in English Literature exams, you'll need to have an extensive knowledge of the books that you study. But you'll also need to prepare yourself for coping with sitting exams in general. The best way to do this is to follow these six steps:

1. Get organised
2. Study in the right environment
3. Manage your exam anxieties
4. Exercise regularly
5. Take breaks and get enough sleep
6. Stay motivated and show resilience

Spending hours glued to your desk is not enough. To do really well and reach your true potential, you'll need to look after yourself and think carefully about getting the most out of your revision time. So far, I've spent a lot of time showing you how to focus on your English skills.

Now I'm going to guide you through the full revision and exam experience. We'll start by thinking about planning your schedule. We'll see what the research says about how you should revise, and how you can look after yourself during this hectic period.

Finally, we'll consider how you can keep going when it seems like things are getting on top of you.

1. Get organised

Researchers have found[1] that students who are organised are more likely to achieve their goals. These students tend to:

- **Create a study plan**
  Starting to revise can seem overwhelming, especially if you've left it till late on in the A-level course. Ideally, you'll have been doing little and often. But if you find yourself feeling overwhelmed, you need

to break the A-level courses down into chunks of learning. A typical week of your English revision timetable may look something like this:

Monday	Tuesday	Wednesday	Thursday	Friday	Saturday	Sunday
'What Would I Give?'	Importance of the Clown in *Doctor Faustus?*	Flashcards: Key critic quotes for *Hamlet*	'Piteous My Rhyme'	'The Lammas Hireling'	Virginia Woolf biographical context	Unseen poetry Practice Question
Re-read Harold Bloom's chapter on *Hamlet*	'Echo'	How do writers present power & vulnerability in *Tess* and *Mrs Dalloway?*	*Mrs Dalloway* narrative voice and structure	Predatory males in *Tess of the D'Urbervilles*	'Babylon the Great'	Flashcards: – Claudius – Ghost & Haunting
Doctor Faustus: context of religious conflict	Unseen poetry Practice Question	'Out of the Bag'	Theme of action and inaction in *Hamlet*		Rossetti key context (female identity)	

- **Check to see how it's going**

  Then, after a week of revision, successful students will monitor their progress and think about what went well and what didn't:

Monday	Tuesday	Wednesday	Thursday	Friday	Saturday	Sunday
'What Would I Give?' ✓	Importance of the Clown in *Doctor Faustus?*	Flashcards: Key critic quotes for *Hamlet*	'Piteous My Rhyme' ✓	'The Lammas Hireling'	Virginia Woolf biographical context ✓	Unseen poetry Practice Question
Re-read Harold Bloom's chapter on *Hamlet*	'Echo' ✓	How do writers present power & vulnerability in *Tess* and *Mrs Dalloway?*	*Mrs Dalloway* narrative voice and structure	Predatory males in *Tess of the D'Urbervilles* ✓	'Babylon the Great'	Flashcards: – Claudius – Ghost & Haunting
Doctor Faustus: context of religious conflict ✓	Unseen poetry Practice Question	'Out of the Bag'	Theme of action and inaction in *Hamlet* ✓		Rossetti key context (female identity) ✓	

Then they'll give themselves reminders and set new targets:

> ### Priorities for next week's revision
> - **Really struggling with 'Out of the Bag' – speak to Mr Roberts on Friday.**
> - **Understand the Clown's role but need better quotes.**
> - **Power/vulnerability thesis statement is weak – needs much more work.**
> - **Was absent when we did 'Babylon the Great' – get Abdul's notes.**

- **Stick to the schedule**

  There will be times when you really don't feel like doing any English revision. The sun's shining outside. There's an amazing new film at the cinema. An electronic device is tempting you.

  Resisting these temptations is the key to success. Ignoring short-term fun for long-term gains is part of the revision process. Nobody really enjoys it but it's an essential part of academic success. Start your revision as soon as you get home from school or college, or as soon as you wake up on a weekend, and it'll be done before you know it. Then you can have guilt-free relaxation time and socialising later on in the evening.

2. Study in the right environment

Where's the best place to study? Library or canteen? In your room or on the kitchen table?

Revising in a really quiet place, on your own or with just one friend, might seem boring. But it's going to give you the **best possible environment for learning**. If you don't have your own room, or live in a hectic house with lots of relatives, then somewhere like a library will be the best place to concentrate.

My students often tell me that they prefer a busier atmosphere. They're fine with noise, they say. But the research into studying environments suggests that they're putting themselves at a disadvantage:

Noise: Learning scientists have found[2] that noise and learning are not a good combination. Background noise interferes with thinking, particularly with teenagers. You might not realise, but studies show noise can also increase stress and frustration.

Music: Listening to your favourite artist while studying might make you feel better but one recent study[3] compared students who revised in a quiet room to those who listened to music. In an exam, those who studied without music outperformed those with music by over 60%.

Mobile phone: Your smartphone can be a huge distraction during study. Research has shown[4] that having your phone on you, even when you aren't using it, has a negative impact on your learning. For that reason, when revising, leave your phone in a different room. Have it with you only during study breaks.

3. Manage your exam anxieties

Feeling nervous about exams is perfectly natural. When things really matter to us, we tend to feel the butterflies in our stomach. But some of us worry a lot more than others. Occasionally, this can interfere with our efforts and stop us performing to our potential.

In my experience, students who have worked hard, in class and at home, tend to feel less stressed about the upcoming exams. Knowing stuff breeds confidence. So, sticking to your revision plan is important.

What else can help me feel less anxious about my exams?

- **Tackle the topics you're most worried about**
  It's tempting, particularly at the start of revision, to spend time on the stuff that you're good at. But it's best to get stuck into the scary things first! Revising a poem you know inside out might feel good but it won't help much in the long run. And you'll always have your nightmare poems lurking in the background.

- **Don't keep procrastinating**
  Finding excuses why you can't revise now will leave you less time to cover everything in the future. It's a damaging cycle that will make you feel worse. Get started and you'll soon be in the habit.

- **Focus on things that are in your control**
  Some things are out of your control. The named poem on the exam paper. The focus of the Shakespeare questions. Whether the grade boundaries are high or low. But there are lots of things you can control. How many times you've read the novels you study. The number of online lectures you watch. The number of practice essays you did on Malvolio. Focus on these things instead of concerning yourself with things that are out of your hands.

- **Accept that events can quickly alter your plans**

  Things don't always run smoothly. Exam boards can change their specifications. Sometimes outside events mean that mock or real exams are postponed or even cancelled. This can feel both unfair and very frustrating. Disruption to your study can cause undue stress and worry. But, in the end, you will get out of a subject what you put in. Knowledge is never wasted, so keep your eye on the bigger picture and don't feel despondent if unexpected things happen.

- **Control your breathing**

  If you feel panicked before or during the exam, close your eyes and take deep breaths. Drink water and focus on positive thoughts.

- **Visualise a positive exam experience**

  Visualisation is a relaxation technique where you imagine calming images in your mind. To help with exam anxieties, picture yourself in the exam room. Sitting at a desk, you're feeling relaxed, determined and confident. Think of it as a calm environment, quiet and a natural place for you to be. Link the exam room to other calm places in your life. Repeat this visualisation regularly throughout the exam period.

4. Exercise regularly

As well as giving you a sense of well-being and helping you sleep better, **physical exercise** might also contribute to better grades. Recent research[5] suggests a link between regular physical activity and brain cell growth. Other studies[6] have also shown a relationship between aerobic exercise and exam performance.

How much exercise should I be aiming for over the revision period?

The government advises that teenagers should make sure they do an average of 60 minutes of physical activity each day. This can be spread out across the day, but the exercise should make you breathe faster and feel warmer.

What kind of exercise counts?

- Running/quick walking
- Sports, such as football, badminton or netball
- Cycling
- Climbing
- Swimming
- Skating
- Practical PE lessons
- Dancing
- Gym workout

When it comes to the exam period, you will be spending lots of time sitting down, revising and doing exams. So if you want to stay healthy and feel good about yourself, then make sure you keep active at other points throughout the day.

5. Take breaks and get enough sleep

Taking breaks during revision is vital. Research has shown[7] that our attention to a study task is limited. After a certain point, we stop taking information in and our performance drops off dramatically. In this study, students who took a couple of brief breaks during the hour of study did better in tests than those who didn't.

So, to stay relaxed and focused, make sure you build the following into your study routine:

- A walk outside
- Getting up and stretching your legs and body
- Go for a healthy snack or drink
- Chat to a friend on the phone
- Do something creative or fun: a spot of doodling or dancing to music

When it comes to **sleep**, the evidence is pretty clear. An important recent study[8] found a direct link between sleep and academic performance. Students who made sure they slept well did better in tests and exams. This shouldn't come as a surprise to you. When you're tired you struggle to concentrate, struggle to remember things, struggle to articulate your ideas. A can of energy drink might seem to wake you up, but the jolt of caffeine will wear off and you'll probably feel even worse afterwards.

This particular study found that students whose sleep was of a better quality, a longer duration, and was more consistent achieved better grades. Importantly, just getting a decent night's sleep the night before the exam wasn't enough. To really feel the benefit – and the researchers found that it could make a 25% difference in results – students needed to have good sleep habits for at least a week, and preferably a month, before exams.

So what sleep patterns are likely to make a difference to your results?

- Get 8–10 hours' sleep per night.
- Keep to a similar routine throughout the week. For example, don't make a habit of staying up very late at weekends, which confuses your body clock.
- In the hour before you go to bed, avoid screen time, loud noises, bright lights, exercise or studying. Your brain needs a calm routine to get ready for sleep. A bath and a dark, quiet bedroom will help settle you for sleep.

6. Stay motivated and show resilience

What are the best ways I can stay motivated during my A-level English Literature revision?

The first thing is to take the chance to notice how much you've improved at English over the course of the A-level. Studies have shown[9] that **performing better at a subject motivates you to want to study it further**. Increasingly, being able to remember more about the texts during retrieval practice should prompt you to keep going. If in doubt, ask your teacher for feedback on your practice paragraphs and essays. Seeing that you're on the right path will encourage you to complete more examples.

Don't give in if you find something difficult. Focusing on your own goals is key. Set yourself small targets along the way and treat yourself for achieving them. Avoid falling into the trap of comparing yourself with others. Stressing about whether someone else will do better than you is a waste of energy. Concentrate instead on knowing more and performing better than you did in previous tests. If you did badly in a mock exam, use this as a learning opportunity, rather than seeing it as a failure. There will inevitably be setbacks throughout your English Literature A-level course. But if you believe in yourself and keep going, even when you really don't feel like it, you'll get the rewards in the end.

66 Top 5 to thrive

1. Create a revision timetable and keep track of how it's going.

2. Limit background noise and other distractions.

3. Focus only on the things that you can control.

4. Take revision breaks, exercise often and get enough sleep.

5. Concentrate on your own gradual improvement and keep going when you find things difficult.

99

A final word – you can do it!

When you first picked up this book, you may well have been struggling to get your head around A-level English Literature revision and may have felt unsure where to start.

So, you've now read this book and have tried out my tips and strategies. Hopefully, you don't feel like that anymore.

If, at any point, you do find yourself worrying about any aspect of your English exams, go back to the relevant section. Re-read the chapter and follow my step-by-step advice again. With plenty of practice, you will get there.

We've been on a journey together. You've followed my advice and you've worked hard. You've got every reason to feel confident when you finally walk into your English exams. Hold your nerve, do your best and make yourself proud.

You can't really revise for A-level English Literature, can you? Well, as you've just proved: yes. Yes, you can!

Mark Roberts

Glossary of terms

This list doesn't include all of the words that can be used in A-level English Literature exams, but you should find it a helpful start.

Alliteration	The repetition of the same consonant sounds in words that are near to each other. e.g. 'O, she doth **t**each the **t**orches **t**o **b**urn **b**right'
Allusion	An unexplained reference to someone or something outside of the text: 1. Biblical – references to people or events from the Bible 2. Literary – references to other novels, plays or poems 3. Classical – references to things like ancient Greek or Roman myths 4. Cultural – references to things like movies, TV programmes, pop music
Analogy	A comparison between two things to help explain something. e.g. 'All the world's a stage/And all the men and women merely players.'
Anaphora	The repetition of a word or phrase at the beginning of lines, sentences or clauses. e.g. '**In every** cry of every Man, **In every** Infants cry of fear…'
Antithesis	The direct opposite of someone or something else. e.g. 'Honest Desdemona is presented as the antithesis of deceitful Iago.'
Aphorism	A short, often witty, sentence which expresses a general truth. e.g. 'There is only one thing in the world worse than being talked about, and that is not being talked about.'
Archetype	A recurring character in literature. e.g. 'In her white clothing, Ophelia fits the female virgin archetype.'
Cacophony	Harsh and unpleasant sounds. e.g. 'With throats unslaked, with black lips baked/Agape they heard me call.'
Caesura	A pause that breaks the rhythm in a line of poetry, created by a comma, full stop, semicolon or dash. e.g. 'She walks in beauty**,** like the night'
Chremamorphism	Giving a person the characteristics of an object. e.g. Basil's dead body in *The Picture of Dorian Gray* is 'the thing… seated in the chair.'
Colloquial language	Communication that is casual, informal and conversational. e.g. "You wanna grab something to eat?"
Conceit	An extended metaphor that runs throughout a poem. e.g. 'In 'Ozymandias', the conceit of the broken, forgotten statue is used to illustrate how a tyrant's power is inevitably temporary.'

Diacope	Repetition where a word or phrase is repeated with one or more words in between. e.g. 'To be, or not to be'
Denouement	The final part of a text in which the plot is tied together and resolved.
Dramatic irony	A situation in a play where the audience is aware of something of which a character (or characters) is not aware.
Dynamic verb	A verb that shows continual or gradual action. e.g. 'The girl **grabbed** the phone from her friend'
Dysphemism	Using harsh or offensive language to make something sound deliberately unpleasant. e.g. 'They have made **worm's meat** of me.'

Enjambment	When a sentence or phrase runs over from one poetic line to the next.
	e.g. 'But huge and mighty forms, that do not live
	    like living men, moved slowly through the mind
	    by day, and were a trouble to my dreams.'

Epanalepsis	Where words or phrases are repeated at the beginning and end of a sentence. e.g. 'Beloved is mine; she is Beloved'
Epizeuxis	Repetition where words or phrases are repeated in immediate succession. e.g. 'words, words, words'
Eponymous	An adjective used where a text is named after the title character(s). e.g. 'In *Othello*, the eponymous general is manipulated by scheming Iago.'
Etymology	The origin of a word. e.g. 'The etymology of the name John is 'God is gracious' (Hebrew)'
Euphemism	A softer word or phrase used to avoid saying an unpleasant or offensive word. e.g. The guards/soldiers in *The Handmaid's Tale* are known as the Angels.
Fin de siècle	Generally means 'end of a century' but often used to describe moral and social concerns about Britain at the end of the 19th century. e.g. 'Dorian Gray's double life reflects fin de siècle fears about transgressive sex.'
Foreshadowing	A structural feature where a writer gives clues about what is to come later in the story.
Form	The type of poem, which can often be defined by its structure (e.g. sonnet, limerick) or its style (e.g. ode, dramatic monologue). Overall poetic form is often categorised in the following four ways: 1. Narrative – poems telling a story, usually involving characters and a plot 2. Lyric – poems expressing strong feelings and emotions 3. Didactic – poems teaching the reader through a moral message 4. Mixed – poems using a combination of the forms above

Hamartia	A fatal flaw leading to the downfall of a tragic hero.
	e.g. 'In *Death of a Salesman*, Willy's hamartia is a deluded perception of himself.'
Hedging language	Language that expresses caution, indirectness or uncertainty.
	e.g. '**It could be argued** that Victor Frankenstein is **perhaps** the novel's real monster.'
Hyperbole	Extreme exaggeration.
	e.g. 'Gatsby is described by Nick as the **son of God**.'
Idiom	Commonly used expression that isn't meant to be taken literally.
	e.g. 'pull someone's leg' to mean play a joke on someone.
Inciting incident	An event or plot point that thrusts the main character(s) to follow their mission.
	e.g. 'The inciting incident in *Hamlet* is the arrival of the ghost of old Hamlet.'
Metatheatre	Theatre which draws attention to its fictional status, often using a play within a play.
	e.g. '*A Midsummer Night's Dream* offers an exquisite example of how metatheatre raises questions about the power of the human imagination.'
Metonymy	The use of a linked term to stand in for an object or concept.
	e.g. 'In the reference to Lear's 'bald crown', the 'crown' represents his kingdom.'
Metre	The basic rhythmic structure of a line within a work of poetry.
Microcosm	A place that acts as a miniature representation of society at large.
	e.g. 'Stanley and Blanche's battle for living space acts as a microcosm for conflict between new and old America in the 1940s and 1950s.'
Motif	A recurring image, idea, or symbol that develops or explains a theme.
	e.g. 'In *Hamlet*, the motif of disease and decay is used to highlight the corruption of the Danish Court.'
Oxymoron	A phrase where two opposite words are joined to create an effect.
	e.g. 'exploding comfortably'
Paradox	An idea or statement that appears to be self-contradictory or make no sense, but which still reveals a hidden truth.
	e.g. 'Hamlet uses the paradox 'I must be cruel, only to be kind' to justify his violent behaviour.'
Pastoral	Texts that are associated with pleasant aspects of rural life and nature.
	e.g. 'The speaker in 'The Prelude' can no longer appreciate nature's pastoral elements: 'no pleasant images of trees/Of sea or sky, no colours of green fields'
Personification	A type of metaphor that makes something non-human seem human.
	e.g. '**dark night strangles** the travelling lamp'
Phallic imagery	An object that represents or resembles an erect penis.

Plosive	An abrupt sound made by closing the mouth then releasing air. Plosive sounds in English are B, P, T, K, G and D. When repeated they often give an impression of harshness and strong emotion.
	e.g. 'ice**d** eas**t** win**d**s tha**t** knive us'
Sentence function	The reason why a sentence has been used by a speaker. There are four types of sentence function:
	1. Imperative – a command or instruction
	2. Interrogative (?) – a question
	3. Exclamatory (!) – expresses strong feelings
	4. Declarative – makes a statement
Synaesthesia	Where a writer uses one sense to describe another.
	e.g. 'Tasting of Flora and the country green.'
Synecdoche	Using a part of something to represent the whole.
	e.g. Using 'Nice **wheels**!' as a compliment about someone's car
Superlative	An adjective that expresses the highest or lowest quality of something.
	e.g. tallest, worst, most embarrassing
Tone	How a writer creates a mood or atmosphere in their writing.
	e.g. 'The speaker's detached tone reveals his ambivalence towards marriage.'
Transitive verb	A verb that accepts one or more objects.
	e.g. 'hold', 'teach', 'tempt'
Tripartite pattern	A list that has three parts.
	e.g. 'foolish, fond old man.'
Trope	Commonly recurring motifs or ideas found in a particular genre or writer's works.
	e.g. 'In *Frankenstein*, Shelley uses the Gothic trope of The Sublime to emphasise the exciting yet dangerous power of nature.'
Volta	Italian for 'turn', this is the part of the poem where the tone or thoughts change.
	e.g. '**Nothing beside remains**. Round the decay
	Of that colossal Wreck, boundless and bare
	The lone and level sands stretch far away.'
Zoomorphism	Giving animal characteristics to humans.
	e.g. 'you'll have your daughter covered with a Barbary horse.'

Endnotes

Chapter 1

Page 4 1 Dunlosky, J., Rawson, K.A., Marsh, E.J., Nathan, M.J., & Willingham, D.T. (2013) 'Improving students' learning with effective learning techniques: promising directions from cognitive and educational psychology', *Psychological Science in the Public Interest*, 14:1, 4–58.

Chapter 10

Page 95 1 Martin, A.J. (2002) 'Motivation and academic resilience: developing a model of student enhancement', *Australian Journal of Education*, 46, 34–49.

Page 97 2 Erickson, L.C. & Newman, R.S. (2017) 'Influences of background noise on infants and children', *Current Directions in Psychological Science*, 26:5, 451–457.

Page 98 3 Currie, H. & Perham, N. (2014) 'Does listening to preferred music improve reading comprehension performance?', *Applied Cognitive Psychology*, 28, 279–284.

Page 98 4 Mendoza, J.S., Pody, B.C., Lee, S., Kim, M., & McDonough, I.M. (2018) 'The effect of cellphones on attention and learning: The influences of time, distraction, and nomophobia', *Computers in Human Behaviour*, 86, 52–60.

Page 99 5 Jack, C.R., Joyner, M.J. & Petersen, R.C. (2020) 'Cardiorespiratory fitness and brain volumes', *Mayo Clinic Proceedings*, 95:1, 6–8.

Page 99 6 For example, Lees, C. & Hopkins, J. (2013) 'Effect of aerobic exercise on cognition, academic achievement, and psychosocial function in children: a systematic review of randomized control trials', *Preventing Chronic Disease*, 10, 174 and Singh, A., Uijtdewilligen, L., Twisk, J.W.R., van Mechelen, W., & Chinapaw, M.J.M. (2012) 'Physical activity and performance at school:a systematic review of the literature including a methodological quality assessment', *JAMA Pediatrics*, 166: 49–55.

Page 100 7 Ariga, A. & Lleras, A. (2011) 'Brief and rare mental "breaks" keep you focused: Deactivation and reactivation of task goals preempt vigilance decrements', *Cognition*, 118:3, 439–443.

Page 100 8 Okano, K., Kaczmarzyk, J.R., Dave, N., Gabrieli, J.D.E. & Grossman, J.C. (2019) 'Sleep quality, duration, and consistency are associated with better academic performance in college students', *NPJ Science of Learning*, 4:16, 1–5.

Page 101 9 Garon-Carrier, G., Boivin, M., Guay, F. et al. (2015) 'Intrinsic motivation and achievement in mathematics in elementary school: A longitudinal investigation of their association', *Child Development* 87:1, 165–175.

Acknowledgements

Extracts and quotations from:

Atonement by Ian McEwan (Vintage Publishing); *A Streetcar Named Desire* by Tennessee Williams (Penguin); *Beloved* by Toni Morrison (Vintage Classics); *Brighton Rock* by Graham Greene (Heinemann); *Death of a Salesman* by Arthur Miller (Penguin); *So Big* by Edna Ferber (Harper Perennial Modern Classics); *The Handmaid's Tale* by Margaret Atwood (Klett Sprachen GmbH); *The Kite Runner* by Khaled Hosseini (Bloomsbury Publishing)

Published by Collins
An imprint of HarperCollins*Publishers*
1 London Bridge Street
London SE1 9GF

HarperCollins*Publishers*
1st Floor, Watermarque Building, Ringsend Road, Dublin 4, Ireland

ISBN: 978-0-00-845545-3

First published 2021

10 9 8 7 6 5 4 3 2 1

British Library Cataloguing in Publication Data.

A CIP record of this book is available from the British Library.

Publisher: Katie Sergeant
Author: Mark Roberts
Project Management: Richard Toms
Cover Design: Sarah Duxbury
Inside Concept Design and Page Layout: Ian Wrigley and James Oxtoby
Production: Karen Nulty
Printed and Bound in the UK using 100% Renewable Electricity at CPI Group (UK) Ltd

MIX
Paper from
responsible source

FSC
www.fsc.org **FSC™ C007454**

This book is produced from independently certified FSC™ paper to ensure responsible forest management.

For more information visit:
www.harpercollins.co.uk/green